NHL ENFORCERS

The Rough and Tough Guys of Hockey

Arpon Basu

OVER TIME BOOKS

© 2006 by OverTime Books
First printed in 2006 10 9 8 7 6 5 4 3 2 1

Printed in Canada

The Publisher: OverTime Books is an imprint of Éditions de la Montagne Verte

Library and Archives Canada Cataloguing in Publication

Basu, Arpon, 1974–
   NHL enforcers : the rough and tough guys of hockey /
Arpon Basu.

Includes bibliographical references.
ISBN-13: 978-1-897277-10-2
ISBN-10: 1-897277-10-5

   1. Hockey—Biography. 2. National Hockey League—
Biography. I. Title.

GV848.5.A1B278 2006   796.962092'2   C2006-904967-X

Project Director: J. Alexander Poulton
Project Editor: Louise Solomita
Cover Image: B.Bennett/Getty Images

PC: P5

Dedication

To the love of my life, Karine, whose patience and understanding while I wrote this makes hcr tougher than all the enforcers profiled in this book.

Contents

Acknowledgments

A very special thanks goes out to the legendary tough guys who took time out of their schedules to be interviewed for this book: John Ferguson, Stu Grimson, Chris Nilan, Dave Schultz and Tony Twist.

An equal degree of gratitude goes to the media relations people who helped put me in touch with these enforcers: Ken Arnold, Tyler Currie, Zack Hill and Dominick Saillant.

I would also like to thank my family for their constant love and support. To Arjun, Dipak, Naomi, Nila and Milo, I love you all dearly.

Introduction

Fighting represents by far the most controversial aspect of hockey, a tradition that has rankled more than a few people who consider it to be a barbaric way to settle on-ice disputes.

But hockey traditionalists will often claim that fighting is the lesser of two evils, and that if it were eliminated from the game the number of high-sticking and slashing infractions would rise sharply. The argument here is that men armed with fists are far less dangerous than ones armed with sticks.

Those same people will also say that fighting has always been a part of the game, which is true, but not in the form we find it today.

In the past, if a star player was being harassed by the opposing team, it was up to him to settle the score himself. Montréal Canadiens legend Maurice "the Rocket" Richard was not only the league's pre-eminent goal scorer, he was also a tough-as-nails fighter who would take matters into his own hands whenever he felt he wasn't being protected by the referees.

But today's form of fighting involves designated enforcers squaring off against the other team's top tough guy, a strategy that first took hold in the 1960s when the Canadiens signed John Ferguson to skate on Jean Béliveau's wing and protect him at all costs.

Although Ferguson was also a skilled hockey player who could put the puck in the net, more and more of today's enforcers have become liabilities on the ice who only receive about five or six minutes of ice time per game from their coaches.

The greatest scorer in NHL history, Wayne Gretzky, may never have been able to roam the ice so liberally if he did not have his own personal bodyguards on the ice. Through the early part of his career with the Edmonton Oilers, the mere presence of Dave Semenko made it so no one entered Gretzky's area code whenever he was on the ice, which gave him the time and space he needed to make those seeing-eye passes right on to the tape of his teammate's stick.

Later in his Oilers career, it was the job of Marty McSorley to keep opponents away from Gretzky. When the Great One was traded to the

Los Angeles Kings in the summer of 1988, he insisted that McSorley be included in the deal to serve as his protector.

Most enforcers who are asked whether fighting is still pertinent in today's NHL point to the fact that, despite the public outcry for it to be banned, it is the part of the game that fans most enjoy.

"Those same people who say fighting should be banned from the NHL," says former St. Louis Blues and Québec Nordiques enforcer Tony Twist, "I don't see them leaving the stands to get popcorn when the fight starts."

The public impression of these designated brawlers is often times the wrong one. When fans watch Dave Schultz and the Broad Street Bullies pillaging their opponents, or the sheer, unbridled joy Chris Nilan got out of fighting, many fans assume that these guys are simply mean and nasty people who weren't hugged enough as children.

But the fact is that in many—if not most—cases, a team's enforcer is also the team's most personable character.

"The most charismatic, entertaining, fun-loving guy you're going to find is your enforcer 80 to 90 percent of the time," Twist says.

A perfect example of this is Todd Ewen, who played the role of policeman for four NHL teams over 11 years, earning himself 1911 penalty minutes in 518 career games by taking on the league's toughest fighters night in and night out.

But away from the rink, Ewen was a gentle soul who became a published author by writing, of all things, storybooks for children.

It is because of this predominant nice-guy trait that many enforcers dread the thought of being forced to fight in order to do their jobs properly.

"The hardest part is psychologically," says reputed Edmonton Oilers tough guy Georges Laraque. "You know, a fight doesn't just start at the game. It starts the night before, two nights before, when you know it's going to happen and you think about it. Doesn't matter what you do, you go to your family, your friends come...and that's all you think about, which is the hardest part about it."

Rob Ray, who sits fifth on the NHL's all-time penalty-minute list with 3207 in 900 games over a 15-year career, says it is far more difficult coping with the reality of an enforcer's role than any other hockey-related stress imaginable.

"The stress of having to score a goal every night is one thing, but the stress of going into a game knowing you're going to have to fight is something totally different," Ray says. "I try to explain that to people and they have a hard time understanding that."

The unfortunate by-product of that stress is that many long-time NHL policemen were forced to turn to alcohol and drugs to help them cope with it.

The list of such cases is very long, but the most tragic one was John Kordic. He was one of the NHL's toughest customers over his seven-year career playing for the Montréal Canadiens, Toronto Maple Leafs, Washington Capitals and Québec Nordiques. But he was also a man who had a great deal of trouble handling the pressure of his role, and Kordic routinely turned to cocaine and alcohol to ease his mind.

Kordic eventually succumbed to those vices, found dead of a cocaine overdose in a Québec City hotel room just before the start of the 1992–93 season.

"He basically killed himself because he couldn't deal with the job," says Twist, who played with Kordic on the Nordiques. "But when John had his head on straight, he was an amazing guy. He was charismatic, smart, the guys loved him."

Brantt Myhres was a journeyman enforcer who had to make a comeback from his own problems with alcohol abuse, and he says the reason he turned to the bottle was also because of the demands of his chosen profession.

"When I broke into the league, I was a 20-year-old fighting 30- and 35-year-old men," Myhres says. "And if you lost three in a row, you were going down [to the minors]. What [alcohol] does is it doesn't allow you to think about the next night. Guys get together [to drink] and they don't talk about fighting...I can't blame [my drinking] on anything, but if I look at all the issues, fighting was definitely a factor."

The debate over whether fighting belongs in hockey has hit its climax in recent years because of two incidents.

Boston Bruins defenceman Marty McSorley, in a poor attempt to engage him in a fight, knocked Vancouver Canucks enforcer Donald Brashear to the ice by whacking him in the head with his stick in February of 2000. Brashear fell and slammed his head on the ice, resulting in a severe concussion for Brashear, and assault charges for McSorley.

Most recently, Canucks forward Todd Bertuzzi pleaded guilty to criminal charges after he sucker-punched Colorado Avalanche forward Steve Moore from behind in March of 2004.

Bertuzzi was attempting to exact revenge for a hit by Moore on Canucks star winger Markus Naslund several weeks earlier, but in so doing Bertuzzi broke Moore's neck and put his NHL career in jeopardy.

The firestorm of criticism for the NHL's tolerance of violent acts following the Bertuzzi-Moore incident was intense, but somewhat unwarranted when it is considered that it was not the first time hockey had witnessed such an act of brutality.

There was Sprague Cleghorn attacking three members of the Ottawa Senators during a game in 1922, leading to his arrest and a $50 fine. Eddie Shore's illustrious career was unfortunately marred by an infamous hit from behind he laid on Ace Bailey that left Bailey with a fractured skull in 1933. Richard's stick chop to the head of Bruins defenceman Hal Laycoe and his attack on a linesman in 1955 led to his suspension for the rest of the season and the playoffs, which eventually resulted in the "Richard Riots" breaking out in the streets of Montréal. And Wayne Maki swung his stick at the head of Bruins tough guy "Terrible" Ted Green in a 1969 exhibition game, leaving him with a fractured skull.

There are, of course, several more instances of extreme violence in the annals of hockey, and the proponents of fighting would argue that these incidents would be far more common if people were forbidden to drop the gloves and settle a score.

This is why many enforcers consider people who want to ban fighting as people who know nothing about the culture of the game and how it is played.

This book makes no attempt to argue, one way or the other, about fighting's value in hockey. But seeing as fighting remains an important part of the game as we know it, this book simply attempts to shine the spotlight on the men who have filled this difficult role with valour over the course of hockey's history.

Chapter One

Eddie Shore

Boston Bruins legend Eddie Shore may have been the greatest combination of elegant skill and ferocious tyranny ever to lace 'em up in the National Hockey League.

Exactly 40 years before Bobby Orr was said to revolutionize the game with his flair and rushing style when he made his debut for the Bruins, it was in fact Shore who introduced the concept of the offensive defenseman to the NHL. But Shore, unlike Orr, had a mean streak that defied comprehension, and it was fueled by his maniacally competitive nature.

Shore was born in 1902 in Fort Qu'Appelle, Saskatchewan, and grew up breaking in his father's stallions on the family farm and hauling grain upwards of 40 miles a day. He enjoyed baseball and soccer as a youngster, and only became interested in hockey when he was about

18 years old because his older brother, Aubrey, told him he could never become a great player. Shore immediately set out to prove his brother wrong, and he improved so quickly that at 22 he was asked to join the Melville Millionaires amateur club for its 1923–24 playoff run.

He spent the next two years playing in the Western Hockey League(WHL), the final one for the Edmonton Eskimos. Shore scored an eye-popping 12 goals for the Eskimos in 1925–26 during an era in which it was unheard of for a defenseman to rush with the puck. His end-to-end rushes, during which he would either skate by players or skate through them, earned Shore the nickname the "Edmonton Express."

The WHL disbanded in 1926, just as the NHL was entering an expansion year. The Bruins had become the first American team in the league in 1924, and now the NHL was adding franchises in Chicago, Detroit and New York to bring its total of U.S. teams to six. This was a dramatic turning point for a league that had been entirely Canadian until 1923. There was a desperate need for a superstar with charisma, someone who could stir the passions of the American fans, who were new to the game. That someone was Shore, whose tremendous skill and violent temperament made him a one-man show on ice.

Shore was among seven WHL players purchased for $50,000 by Bruins owner and grocery tycoon Charles Adams, and it would quickly prove to be the soundest investment Adams made since the $15,000 expansion fee he had paid two years earlier. Shore's innovative style of offensive play was a hit with Boston fans, and his tough and abrasive nature didn't take long to emerge.

During his rookie season, Shore got into a violent scrap with veteran Billy Coutu, who just happened to be Shore's teammate. The dust-up got so violent that Shore's ear was nearly severed, and he wound up spending the rest of the day looking all over Boston for a doctor who would be willing to sew it back on instead of amputating it.

"I was just a farm boy who didn't want his looks messed up," Shore joked later. "I made him change the last stitch; he would have left a scar!"

Although a Boston Globe writer once referred to Shore as the Babe Ruth of hockey because of the way he was popularizing the game, a better comparison would be to call him the Ty Cobb of hockey—supremely talented, viciously mean-spirited, and mildly disturbed.

Shore scored 12 goals his rookie season—an unprecedented number for an NHL defenseman—and also racked up 130 minutes in penalties, second-most in the league. The following year in 1927–28, Shore set a new NHL record with 165 penalty minutes while scoring 11 goals, the second of five straight seasons in which he topped the 10-goal plateau.

Shore's toughness was found not only in the way he defended himself with his fists and his stick. He would routinely play upwards of 55 minutes during a 60-minute contest. In 1928–29, Shore would lead the Bruins to an undefeated playoff run to give Boston its first Stanley Cup championship.

The following year, however, Shore would establish a far more notorious league mark that is almost sure to never to be broken. On November 23, 1929, Shore was assessed five fighting majors in a single game against the Montréal Maroons. He began the carnage with a bout against Buck Boucher, and as soon as that one was over, Shore butt-ended Dave Trottier. That night, Shore had his pick of challengers and he took them all on, to the point where referees had to put a halt to the game in the third period. Shore, Boucher and the Maroons' Albert "Babe" Siebert were all hospitalized, but Shore's list of injuries was the longest. He had a broken nose, four missing teeth, two black eyes and a concussion, among other things.

But to Shore, that wasn't much worse than how he felt after nearly every game he played, according to his former teammate Milt Schmidt.

"He was bruised head to toe after every game," Schmidt recalled. "Everybody was after him. They figured if they could stop Eddie Shore, they could stop the Bruins."

Two years later, in 1931–32, Shore would have the finest statistical season of his career with 8 goals, 27 assists and 102 penalty minutes. His 35 points that season tied him for 10th in the league with Canadiens legend Howie Morenz, among others, and he capped the year by becoming the first defenseman to win the Hart Trophy as the NHL's most valuable player. Shore would win the award three more times, in 1935, 1936 and 1938, and he remains the only NHL defenseman ever to win the Hart Trophy four times.

Unfortunately, Shore's most famous moment was one of great tragedy for the NHL. On December 12, 1933, Shore's Bruins were hosting the Toronto Maple Leafs. During the game's second period, Shore took off on one of his trademark end-to-end rushes. Just as he entered the Toronto zone, he was tripped by Maple Leafs star defenseman Francis "King" Clancy. Shore was enraged, and immediately looked for someone to pay the price for Clancy's act. However, Clancy had already taken off to launch a counter-attack and Toronto forward Ace Bailey was the unfortunate soul who was closest to Shore as he picked himself up off the ice.

Shore skated straight toward the unsuspecting Bailey and leveled him with a vicious hit from behind. Since Bailey had no idea the blow was coming, he couldn't brace himself and went sprawling to the ice.

Toronto assistant general manager Frank Selke remembers seeing the incident from the front row of the press box that night.

"Shore arose and slowly started back to his end of the playing arena," Selke later wrote in his memoirs. "He was behind (Red) Horner and Bailey. Whether he mistook Bailey for Clancy, or whether he was annoyed by his own futility and everything in general, we will never know. But we all saw Shore put his head down and rush at top speed. He struck Bailey across the kidneys with his right shoulder and with such force that it upended Bailey in a backward somersault, while the powerful Shore kept right on going."

Immediately after checking on his fallen team-mate, Maple Leafs defenseman Reginald "Red" Horner skated over to Shore and clocked him with a quick right to the jaw, knocking the Bruins legend out cold.

Bailey began convulsing once he arrived in the Leafs dressing room, and his head was packed in ice before he was rushed to the hospital, where it was discovered he had suffered a concussion and a fractured skull. Doctors performed two risky brain surgeries on Bailey over the next six days, and even then were uncertain whether or not he would be able to live a normal life. Meanwhile, Shore was being interviewed by Boston police about the incident, and it was made clear to him that if Bailey died, he would be charged with manslaughter.

Bailey was so close to dying after the second operation that a priest was brought in to read his last rites, but his condition improved dramatically the next morning and within two weeks, he was on the road to a full recovery. Although Bailey would never play professionally again, he would lead a long life, dying at the age of 88 in 1992.

The incident had a great psychological impact on Shore, but an even bigger impact on the NHL. After serving his 16-game suspension, Shore returned to the Bruins, but he wasn't nearly the same player.

Two months after the incident, a fundraiser was organized in Toronto for Bailey in what was the

NHL's first all-star game. Before the opening puck drop, Shore tentatively skated over to Bailey and offered him his hand. Bailey accepted the offer and gave Shore a firm handshake that made it clear there were no hard feelings. That forgiveness may have been what Shore needed, because he went on to win back-to-back Hart trophies the following two years and won his fourth and final MVP award in 1938.

He would lead the Bruins to their second Stanley Cup championship in 1939, and played only one more season in the NHL before finishing his playing career with the American Hockey League team he purchased, the Springfield Indians.

By the end of Shore's rough yet graceful career, he had taken 978 stitches, suffered 14 broken noses and five broken jaws. He also spent 1037 minutes in the penalty box over his 14 NHL seasons, an impressive figure today, but an astronomical one in the 1930s.

Most importantly, Shore created an entire generation of hockey fans in the United States with his ruthless style and electrifying rushes up the ice. If there were one person responsible for popularizing Canada's game south of the border, it would have to be Eddie Shore.

Eddie Shore

Position: Defence
Date of birth : November 25, 1902
Place of birth: Fort Qu'Appelle, Saskatchewan

Season	Team	Lge	Regular Season					Playoffs				
			GP	G	A	Pts	PIM	GP	G	A	Pts	PIM
1924–25	Regina Capitals	WCHL	24	6	0	6	75					
1925–26	Edmonton Eskimos	WCHL	30	12	3	15	92					
1926–27	Boston Bruins	NHL	41	12	6	18	130					
1927–28	Boston Bruins	NHL	44	11	6	17	165					
1928–29	Boston Bruins	NHL	39	12	7	19	96					
1929–30	Boston Bruins	NHL	43	12	19	31	105					
1930–31	Boston Bruins	NHL	44	15	16	31	105					
1931–32	Boston Bruins	NHL	44	9	13	22	80					
1932–33	Boston Bruins	NHL	48	8	27	35	102					
1933–34	Boston Bruins	AHL	30	2	10	12	57					
1934–35	Boston Bruins	NHL	49	7	26	33	32					
1935–36	Boston Bruins	NHL	46	3	16	19	61	2	1	2	2	12
1936–37	Boston Bruins	NHL	19	3	1	4	12	–	–	–	–	–
1937–38	Boston Bruins	NHL	47	3	14	17	42	3	0	1	1	6
1938–39	Boston Bruins	NHL	46	4	14	18	37	12	0	4	4	19
1939–40	Boston Bruins	NHL	4	2	1	3	4	–	–	–	–	–
1939–40	New York Americans	NHL	10	2	3	5	9	3	0	2	2	2
1939–40	Springfield Indians	AHL	15	1	14	15	18					
1940–41	Springfield Indians	AHL	56	4	13	17	6					
1941–42	Springfield Indians	AHL	35	5	12	17	61					
1942–43	Buffalo Bisons	AHL	1	0	0	0	0					
	NHL Totals		553	105	179	284	1037	20	1	8	9	39

Eddie Shore finished among the top 10 in the NHL in penalty minutes in each of his first nine seasons with the Boston Bruins, and he was in the top four for five straight seasons to start his career. However, he only led the NHL in penalty minutes once over his long and mean career, in 1927–28.

Chapter Two

John Ferguson

Although fighting has always been a part of hockey, the concept of using enforcers is relatively new to the game. Before the advent of the designated tough guy, star players often had to protect themselves against cheap shots and errant sticks. Many argue that the NHL's first enforcer was used in the early 1960s when Montréal Canadiens general manager Frank Selke decided he needed someone to watch over his franchise player, Jean Béliveau.

Selke found that man in John Ferguson, a brawler from the West Coast who prided himself on being the meanest and nastiest player on the ice. For eight seasons with the Canadiens, Ferguson fought anyone who dared challenge him and, more importantly, anyone who ventured too close to Béliveau. Even though the team was stacked with stars, many fans believe the Habs would never have been able to win five Stanley Cups over that period were it not for Ferguson patrolling Béliveau's wing.

His menacing nature on the ice was instilled by something he saw as a 16-year-old growing up in the East Hastings neighborhood of Vancouver, British Columbia.

The teenage Ferguson was already tough. An only child, Ferguson's father died when he was just nine years old, and he suddenly became the man of his household. With his mother logging heavy hours as a floor lady and seamstress at a local factory, Ferguson learned to be responsible at a young age.

"I had to do everything on my own," Ferguson says. "I'd come home and get the potatoes ready and our dinner ready, then she'd come home from work, and that's how we grew up together."

Despite his domestic responsibilities, Ferguson was always involved in sports, and he was a tremendous athlete in almost anything he tried. At the age of 12, Ferguson laid the groundwork for his future status as the NHL's most ferocious fighter when he began boxing at the Gibbs Boys Club. He was also an elite lacrosse player in Vancouver, and might very well have played that game at a professional level had he not discovered hockey when he was 14.

Although he was a late arrival to the game, Ferguson took to it immediately and began spending all his free time at the rink. When he wasn't playing, Ferguson would be there to collect 25 cents every time he cleaned a sheet of ice, and he was also a stick boy for the Western Hockey League's Vancouver Canucks.

One night during the 1954–55 season, when he was 16, Ferguson watched his Canucks take on the Edmonton Flyers, who boasted one of the toughest guys in the league, defenseman Larry Zeidel.

Vancouver's best player that season was Phil Maloney, who at one point wound up in the penalty box with Zeidel (players from both teams used to sit in the same penalty box). Suddenly, to Ferguson's absolute horror, Zeidel turned and sucker-punched Maloney right in the face. Not only that, but none of Maloney's Canucks teammates came to his defense. Ferguson was disgusted.

"That always stayed in the back of my mind," Ferguson says. "I told myself that nobody would ever have to worry about me not protecting my teammates."

In 1956, Ferguson was 18 years old and one of the top young players in Vancouver when he packed his bags and got on a train to Melville, Saskatchewan, where he would play with the Junior A Melville Millionaires, under coach William "Legs" Fraser, for two seasons, serving as team captain in his final year.

Ferguson was a good enough student to receive scholarship offers to play hockey at North Dakota and Colorado College, but he was also invited to the Canucks' training camp that fall, and decided to play for their minor-league International Hockey League team, the Fort Wayne Komets.

After one season in Fort Wayne, Ferguson was signed in 1960 by the Cleveland Barons of the American Hockey League—just one rung below the NHL. At that point, Larry Zeidel had become a fixture as the enforcer of the AHL's Hershey Bears, and Ferguson had never forgotten what Zeidel did to Phil Maloney in Vancouver all those years ago. Ferguson already had a reputation as a tough guy by then, and just before the young fighter was to play Hershey for the first time, Zeidel—not realizing how much Ferguson despised him—tried to approach the budding enforcer.

"I remember going into a club in Hershey," Ferguson says, "and Zeidel came up to me and said, 'If you don't bother me, I won't bother you.' I just said, 'I'm sorry, but I'll play my game and you play yours.' "

When the Barons and the Bears faced off a couple of nights later, Ferguson avenged Maloney by pounding on Zeidel first on the ice, and again in the penalty box moments later. The message Ferguson sent that night spread throughout the AHL, and it wasn't long before he was considered a man not to be messed with.

In his final AHL season, 1962–63, 24-year-old Ferguson finished third in the league in goals with 38 and second in penalty minutes with 179 in 72 games played. That combination of skill and toughness made it so Ferguson had his pick of teams when it came time to decide where he would continue his career in the NHL.

Legendary Montréal Canadiens head coach Hector "Toe" Blake and scout Floyd Curry saw Ferguson in the 1963 AHL playoffs, and Curry convinced Canadiens GM Frank Selke Sr. to offer the fiery winger a contract. Ferguson also received offers from the Boston Bruins and New York Rangers, but in his mind the decision was obvious, and he signed with the Canadiens for

$7250, more than doubling his salary from the previous season.

The reason Selke and Blake were so eager to get Ferguson into the Canadiens lineup was that Montréal had become a bit of a pushover in the six-team NHL. Though Montréal had extraordinarily talented players, led by superstars Jean Béliveau, Henri Richard and Bernie "Boom Boom" Geoffrion, the Canadiens lacked the toughness to stand up to some of the more brutal teams in the league.

The year before Ferguson's arrival, Béliveau had one of the worst seasons of his career, scoring only 18 goals and failing to record one point per game for a second straight year. Béliveau was a well-established superstar by then, but teams began roughing up "Le Gros Bill" night after night to try to shake him off his game, and the Canadiens lacked an enforcer fierce enough to act as a deterrent.

Before Ferguson's first regular-season game with the Canadiens, Blake walked over to the rookie winger and told him he'd be playing on a line with Béliveau and Geoffrion. "You protect the two big guys," Blake told him. Ferguson knew exactly what he meant.

The Canadiens were facing the Boston Bruins on opening night of the 1963–64 season, and

Blake picked Béliveau's line to start the game. The Bruins sent out their tough guy, the notorious "Terrible" Ted Green, who immediately started jawing at Ferguson. The puck dropped, and the rookie decided right then and there that it was time to make his mark in the National Hockey League. A mere 12 seconds into his first game, Ferguson dropped the gloves with Green and sent a message.

"I had a reputation from the American League, and he had a reputation in the National League. So I figured I might as well start at the top of the mountain," Ferguson says. "I just never let up after that."

Ferguson's arrival gave Béliveau the room he had been lacking the previous two years. If anyone so much as breathed on the star player, Ferguson made certain it didn't happen again. But he was not just a fist-flailing goon. Although his hands were larger than the average man's and they could inflict ridiculous amounts of pain and suffering, they also had a scoring touch.

Ferguson had two goals and an assist in that first game to go with his fight with Green, giving him the cherished "Gordie Howe" hat trick of a goal, an assist and a fight. Of course, playing on Béliveau's wing opposite Geoffrion provided many scoring chances, but not every enforcer could necessarily finish those chances with a goal. Ferguson did more often than not.

Ferguson was in fact sitting near the top of the league's scoring list when a gruesome accident in Boston cut out a chunk of his rookie season. Ferguson got into a scrap with Bruin Ed Westfall. Ferguson had a reputation for continuing to throw punches until the linesmen moved in, whether his opponent was on his skates or not. In this case, that ruthlessness landed Ferguson in a bit of trouble.

"I knocked him down and went to punch him again, but he put his skate up and I punched right through his skate," Ferguson recalls. "My thumb was hanging on by its skin."

Ferguson was rushed to a Boston hospital, and doctors managed to sew the thumb back on. The rookie missed the next 18 games of the 1963–64 season before coming back to finish the year with a steel cast. After the season ended, doctors had to operate on Ferguson's thumb again because he couldn't move it.

But he was back the following season, and the Canadiens were tied at two games apiece with the Chicago Blackhawks in the 1965 Stanley Cup finals when Ferguson dropped the gloves with Chicago tough guy Eric Nesterenko. What followed was one of the most brutal incidents in the history of the Stanley Cup playoffs. Ferguson knocked Nesterenko cold with one punch. The Canadiens easily won the fifth game 6–0, and went on to win the franchise's 13th Stanley Cup with a 4–0 win in game seven. That would be the first of four consecutive Stanley Cups for the Canadiens, and it would not be the last time Ferguson used his fists to shift the momentum in a playoff series.

Montréal was matched up against "Terrible" Ted Green's Boston Bruins in the first round of the 1968 playoffs, and fans and media alike believed whoever managed to physically intimidate their opponent would emerge victorious. It was the type of situation Ferguson lived for. In game one of the series, Ferguson dropped the gloves with Green, and it wasn't long before Green dropped down to the ice after weathering a series of vicious blows. The Canadiens never looked back after that fight, sweeping the series in four games. Ferguson said the Bruins lost their aggressiveness after he so convincingly pounded their toughest player, and years later, a Canadiens scout from the time confirmed that feeling.

"If Ferguson would have lost that fight," Ron Caron said, "the series would have probably gone the other way."

Though Ferguson never fought as often as some of the league's other enforcers—he only led the league in fighting majors twice in his eight-year playing career—it was the way he fought that made him such a legend. In fact, the main reason he didn't pile up that many fighting majors is because, frankly, no one particularly wanted to fight him.

"John Ferguson had no conscience," former NHL coach and Hockey Night in Canada broadcaster Harry Neale once said. "Even some of the toughest players have had a conscience. They knew when they had gone too far, and they were sorry they did. Not John Ferguson. A lot of guys who fight like the fighting, but they don't want to hurt anyone. Ferguson would hurt you."

Ferguson has often said that his purpose was "to be the meanest son of a bitch in the National Hockey League." It would be difficult to find someone to say that Ferguson failed to attain that goal.

But Ferguson didn't leave his nasty temperament behind when he left the rink. He was adamant that he would never fraternize with opposing players, even in the off-season. If someone was holding a golf tournament and players from other teams were invited, Ferguson would politely decline. Once, while eating dinner, Ferguson got up and walked out of a restaurant as soon as he saw Toronto Maple Leafs agitator Eddie Shack come in. Ferguson even acted this way with former teammates. He remembers when the Canadiens traded his close friend Bryan "Bugsy" Watson to the Detroit Red Wings after the 1964–65 season.

"I remember one night we were in Detroit, I got into a scrap with Gary Bergman and (Watson) jumped me from behind," Ferguson remembers with a laugh. "God, he really made me mad. So we used to go to the Lindell Athletic Club after games in Detroit for a couple of beers and such, and I jumped right over the goddamn jukebox to get at him. But we're still the closest of friends now."

Ferguson's reputation as a pugilist was so respected that early in his career he was offered the chance to fight an exhibition bout with Canadian heavyweight champion George Chuvalo—a man who twice went the distance with Muhammad Ali without once being knocked down.

"At that time, I was pretty cocky in life," Ferguson says. "I was going to do it."

If Canadiens GM Sam Pollock hadn't stepped in and put a stop to the event, Ferguson might very well have entered that ring in Toronto, and who knows what would have happened.

After only eight seasons with the Canadiens, Ferguson decided in 1971 that he had had enough. He was making more money with his Montréal clothing business than he was playing for the Canadiens. More importantly, a vision of doom had started to creep into Ferguson's mind.

"That's really the thing that made me retire," Ferguson explains, "I thought I was going to hurt somebody badly in a fight." Perhaps Neale was wrong about Ferguson not having a conscience.

Pollock, however, wasn't going to let his policeman leave without a fight. Béliveau also retired following the 1970–71 season, leaving the Canadiens captaincy vacant. Pollock, in an effort to entice Ferguson to change his mind, offered him the honored post. Ferguson politely declined and began concentrating on his clothing business, but it wasn't long before he began having doubts.

"I looked back a year or so later," he says, "and thought how it would have been a great thrill to be the captain of the Montréal Canadiens."

It wasn't long, however, before Ferguson was back in the hockey world, as he was selected to serve as an assistant coach for Team Canada in the legendary 1972 Summit Series against the Soviet Union. Late in the eighth and deciding game of the series in Moscow, with the contest tied 5–5 and the series tied at three games for each side and one tie, Ferguson was nervously watching the game from behind the Canadian bench.

Ferguson remembers several members of the Soviet team's braintrust coming to see him during that game to tell him they would claim victory in the series if the game remained tied because the Soviets had scored one more goal than Canada. Ferguson, enraged at the idea, didn't have time to respond.

"They no sooner finished saying that," Ferguson says, "when [Canada's] Paul Henderson scored the winning goal."

That memorable experience with Team Canada led Ferguson into his second career in hockey, one that continues to this day. He became general manager and coach of the New York Rangers in 1976, and moved on to run the Winnipeg Jets for 11 seasons, from 1978–89, winning a World Hockey Association title in his first year with the Jets and leading the team through its first 10 seasons in the NHL.

Curiously, Ferguson did not emphasize the rougher aspects of the game as a front-office type, actually leading the charge toward drafting and using smaller European players. Ferguson's trip to Russia for the 1972 Summit Series opened his eyes to all the talent in Sweden, Finland, the former Czechoslovakia and Russia.

Ferguson drafted Swedish great Thomas Steen for the Jets, and he also used the 10th overall pick in the 1988 entry draft to select Finnish superstar Teemu Selanne.

Since leaving the Jets, Ferguson has worked as director of player personnel for the Ottawa Senators for three seasons before joining the San Jose Sharks' front office in 1996.

Ferguson's mark on the game remains evident to this day in all the bruising NHL tough guys who have a specific role to fill and play no more than six or seven minutes a night. Each and every one of them owes Ferguson a great deal of thanks for creating a position that, before he came along, never existed.

John Ferguson

Position: Right wing
Date of birth: September 5, 1938
Place of birth: Vancouver, BC

Season	Team	Lge	Regular Season					Playoffs				
			GP	G	A	Pts	PIM	GP	G	A	Pts	PIM
1959–60	Fort Wayne Komets	IHL	68	32	33	65	126					
1960–61	Cleveland Barons	AHL	62	13	21	34	126	–	–	–	–	–
1961–62	Cleveland Barons	AHL	70	20	21	41	146	6	2	2	4	6
1962–63	Cleveland Barons	AHL	72	38	40	78	179	7	3	3	6	17
1963–64	Montréal Canadiens	NHL	59	18	27	45	125	7	0	1	1	25
1964–65	Montréal Canadiens	NHL	9	17	27	44	156	13	3	1	4	28
1965–66	Montréal Canadiens	NHL	65	11	14	25	153	10	2	0	2	44
1966–67	Montréal Canadiens	NHL	67	20	22	42	177	10	4	2		22
1967–68	Montréal Canadiens	NHL	61	15	18	33	117	13	3	5	8	25
1968–69	Montréal Canadiens	NHL	71	29	23	52	15	14	4	3	7	80
1969–70	Montréal Canadiens	NHL	48	19	13	32	139	–	–	–	–	–
1970–71	Montréal Canadiens	CAHL	60	16	14	30	162	18	4	6	10	36
	NHL Totals		500	145	158	303	1214	85	20	18	38	260

John Ferguson finished in the NHL's top 10 in penalty minutes in all but one of his eight seasons with the Montréal Canadiens, and he led the league with 177 in 1966–67.

Chapter Three

Bob Probert

Over the course of his 16 NHL seasons, Bob Probert was the poster child for NHL enforcers in more ways than one. On one hand, he was a menacing figure in the lineups of the Detroit Red Wings and Chicago Blackhawks from 1985 to 2002, a man the opposing team had to account for and one who appeared in the nightmares of players who knew they would be facing a flurry of Probert's fists.

"When you went in to play Chicago or Detroit, you always talked about Bob Probert," fellow heavyweight Lyle Odelein said when Probert announced his retirement in 2002. "All the younger guys probably couldn't sleep the night before because they were so excited to get to fight him. Everybody wanted to say they fought Bob Probert and came out alive."

On the other hand, Probert was also an example of how the role of designated peacekeeper can force many to seek solace in a bottle or drugs. Unfortunately, Probert's public battle with drug and alcohol abuse was one that several NHL enforcers have fought, and in some cases, those battles ended in tragedy.

But it is a tribute to Probert that, despite his repeated relapses and trips to rehab clinics, he never allowed his demons to fully consume him. Probert's fighting style in the NHL was to let a guy get a few punches in before unleashing his own barrage of rights and lefts. His history of substance abuse followed much the same pattern, with his booze and cocaine habits taking the early rounds, while Probert fought back to come out on top in the end.

But often lost in the predominant talk about Probert's off-ice problems and his on-ice fisticuffs is the fact that the kid from Windsor, Ontario, was not only the league's best and most feared fighter, he was also a pretty good hockey player. Probert displayed his rare combination of skills in his first season of junior with the Brantford Alexanders of the Ontario Hockey League, getting 28 points and 133 penalty minutes as a 17-year-old rookie. A few days after his 18th birthday in 1983, the Detroit Red Wings took Probert in the NHL draft with the 46th overall pick.

It was pretty clear what the Red Wings were looking for in the draft that year. After picking center Steve Yzerman fourth overall and actually disappointing some in the Detroit area that they missed out on American star Pat LaFontaine, the Red Wings took Probert in the third round, fellow "Bruise Brother" Joey Kocur in the fifth round, and Stu "the Grim Reaper" Grimson in the 10th round. The three brawlers would eventually combine for just under 8000 penalty minutes over the course of their careers.

Probert and Kocur made their mark in Detroit during the 1985–86 season. Kocur, a year older than Probert, already had a season in the pros under his belt and was therefore the more active of the two that year with 377 penalty minutes in only 59 games.

Probert, however, immediately displayed a decent scorer's touch to go with his ability to punch right through a wall. He scored 8 goals with 13 assists for 21 points in 44 games his rookie year, adding 186 penalty minutes for good measure.

More importantly, Probert's first NHL fight showed that he would become one of the most entertaining enforcers in league history because of the length and sheer ferocity of his bouts. On November 11, 1985, Probert's Red Wings faced the Vancouver Canucks and their rookie scrapper, Craig Coxe, a onetime Red Wings draft pick. It was only Coxe's 12th career game so he had something to prove, while Probert was looking to establish himself in the fraternity of NHL scrappers after being called up from the minors.

The ensuing fight that night in Vancouver has gone down in NHL lore, equaled only by the rematch later on in the 1985–86 season in Detroit. Both duels featured little grappling and a flurry of punches. Hockey's most vocal fighting activist, former Boston Bruins head coach Don Cherry, once counted the number of punches thrown during the second bout between Probert and Coxe for one of his *Rock 'Em Sock 'Em* videos. Cherry counted 71 punches between the two in only 50 seconds, the fight ending with Probert landing two nasty uppercuts directly to Coxe's face just before the linesmen stepped in. Highlights of the two fights were widely seen around the league that year, and Probert's status as one of the NHL's elite fighters was well on its way to taking hold.

In 1987–88, Probert had the best season of his career, possibly the best season ever by an enforcer. Probert led the league with 398 penalty minutes—the sixth-highest total ever—but he also contributed offensively that year, playing on Steve Yzerman's right wing and earning an invitation to the NHL All-Star game. He scored 29 goals with 33 assists for 62 points in 74 games, a combination of toughness and touch never before seen in the NHL.

"You can say Probie was the toughest guy ever to play, but I don't think people saw what a great person he was," said Chris Simon, a fellow enforcer who, like Probert, also had some skill for the game. "He's a really good guy in addition to being the toughest guy around. Guys like him are hard to come by. You look at what he did when he had 29 goals and 398 penalty minutes. I mean, I don't think you'll ever see that happen again."

The Coxe fight had such an impact on Cherry that he used his soapbox as a commentator on "Coach's Corner" during a CBC *Hockey Night in Canada* broadcast that year to discuss it, expressing his appreciation for the young Red Wings tough guy. As the years went on in Detroit and Probert continued beating the league's heavyweights, Cherry decided Probert was the new measuring stick for up-and-coming NHL enforcers.

Partly because of Cherry's statement, Probert was challenged virtually every time he played, and he rarely said no. Toronto Maple Leafs enforcer Tie Domi is among the legions of Probert opponents who got their big break by beating him. Domi's legendary bout was at Madison Square Garden in 1992.

"I've always said, 'I'm glad I'm not him,' " tough guy Peter Worrell once said. "I think Don Cherry did him a disservice by saying that if you wanted to be a tough guy, you had to fight Probie. After that, every guy who came up did because he was the benchmark to see if you were a real guy or a phony. He went to battle every night in every game; he had a lot of guts."

But with Probert's status as a hockey star in a city affectionately called Hockeytown came the problems that often follow success at such a young age. Probert was arrested several times for driving under the influence, going in and out of rehab programs for alcohol abuse throughout the early years of his career in Detroit. Probert became so unpredictable that Red Wings management assigned assistant coach Colin Campbell the task of shadowing the troubled enforcer during the 1988–89 season.

One time early in that season, Probert was working out at Windsor Arena while serving a suspension and undergoing treatment for alcoholism. Probert left the ice at one point, claiming he would be back in one minute. A few minutes later, Campbell went looking for Probert and found him smoking a cigarette in the locker room and talking to a fan. Campbell was so enraged, he and Probert went to blows, and Campbell showed up for work the next day with two black eyes.

On March 2, 1989, however, Probert's life as he knew it changed forever. He was caught at the border crossing the Detroit Windsor Tunnel with a 14.3-gram bag of cocaine in his underwear. That offence earned him a three-month stay at the Federal Medical Center in Rochester, Minnesota, another three months in a halfway house and a lifetime ban from the NHL. After serving his sentence, Probert received a temporary work permit from the U.S. government, and his NHL ban was lifted a month later in March of 1990. But because of his brush with the law, and more specifically his attempt to enter the country with drugs, the U.S. immigration department told Probert that if he left the country, there was no guarantee he would be allowed back.

Probert, therefore, was not allowed to play games in Canada, or even cross the river to visit his hometown of Windsor until a deal was struck with the U.S. immigration department in 1992. He played his first game in Canada at Toronto's Maple Leaf Gardens on December 9, 1992, almost four years to the day after his last game in Canada.

"It was a great feeling coming through the tunnel," Probert told Toronto reporters that day. "One of the tough things was that Windsor is only across the Detroit River. I could see it every day when I went down to the rink to practice. It was a little tough seeing it every day and knowing it was that close, but yet it seemed so far away."

Probert vowed at that time to be a changed man, one who had learned his lesson, and hoped he could build a solid foundation for a sober life. But Probert was claimed by addiction once more on July 15, 1994, when he crashed his motorcycle in a Detroit suburb. Not only was Probert found to have a blood-alcohol level three times over the legal limit, there was also cocaine found in his system. All of a sudden, Probert was back to square one. The Red Wings had grown tired of Probert's off-ice problems, and the motorcycle accident was the last straw. Detroit put him on waivers only four days later.

"He was popular and charismatic, but I think the fans can understand that 7 goals and 29 points is not high performance," Red Wings senior vice-president Jimmy Devellano said. "We're looking for committed, dedicated people who want to play and play hard."

Probert, however, did not remain jobless very long. Division rivals the Chicago Blackhawks wasted little time—three days, to be exact—before signing Probert to a four-year contract worth $6.6 million.

"The day after the accident, I was lying in my hospital bed, my wife was seven months pregnant, it wasn't a pretty sight," Probert said. "Everything was in limbo—my career, my life. I would have to say that was the lowest point... But they still signed me, a week after the accident, which showed me a lot."

Probert missed the entire 1994–95 season recovering from his injury and getting treatment for his relapse into substance abuse. During his first game with the Blackhawks of the 1995–96 season, against the Oilers, he was thrown out for instigating a fight.

Probert enjoyed a resurgence of sorts that season, posting solid totals of 19 goals and 21 assists with 237 penalty minutes in 78 games. But his resurgence was not limited to the ice.

The Blackhawks watched as Probert appeared to turn his personal life around, to the point where management began pairing the team's younger players in rooms with him while on the road so that they could benefit from the wise life lessons the hardened Probert had to offer.

"In the past, I figured I could drink a little here, drink a little there," Probert said early in his tenure with the Blackhawks. "Every time I tried that, it had the same ending, and it wasn't good. I had to come to terms with that, and I believe I have now. [The counselors] say it's got to be this way or no way. I would try to cut corners, take the middle road. But it was cut and dried. I took me a while to understand that and accept that."

Probert played seven seasons with Chicago without any major incidents, and he had some significant career milestones in a Blackhawks uniform. He scored the last goal ever at Toronto's Maple Leaf Gardens in 1999, and in 2000, he became the sixth NHL player in history to pass the 3000-penalty-minute mark. But the years of battling and taking punches took their toll, and Probert called it quits in November 2002 to take a job with the Blackhawks broadcast team.

"It's not easy, but it's exciting to step into something else in the game instead of not doing anything," Probert said at the time he made the move. "I felt good, but unfortunately I didn't fit into their plans here."

As soon as word spread around the league of his retirement, accolades and tributes began to fall like rain from every tough guy in the league.

"In my mind, he's the greatest fighter of all time," enforcer Georges Laraque said. "To last as long as he did with all the young guns coming in, trying to make a name for themselves by fighting him...he's almost 40 and he never turned anybody down. He's the all-time warrior."

Unfortunately, Probert couldn't keep fighting his battle against alcoholism, and in 2003, he voluntarily re-entered the NHL Players Association's substance abuse program.

"The adjustment from my last year of playing to my first year of not playing was pretty tough," Probert said. "One of the biggest adjustments for me is trying to stay busy."

One of the ways Probert accomplished that once he got out of rehab was to spend more time with his wife, Dani, and their four children back home in Windsor. Though he lived through some difficult times over his 16 seasons in the NHL, Probert accomplished what few people ever do—he became exactly what he had set out to become.

"How do I want to be remembered?" Probert said when his retirement was made official. "I guess just as a hard-nosed player who played hard every night, gave it his all, got some points and got in some scraps."

Those scraps were some of the most memorable in hockey history and assured Probert of a legacy he can live with, hopefully in full sobriety.

Bob Probert

Position: Left wing
Date of birth: June 5, 1965
Place of birth: Windsor, Ontario

Season	Team	Lge	Regular Season GP	G	A	Pts	PIM	Playoffs GP	G	A	Pts	PIM
1982–83	Brantford Alexanders	OHL	51	12	16	28	133	8	2	2	4	23
1983–84	Brantford Alexanders	OHL	65	35	38	73	189	6	0	3	3	16
1984–85	Hamilton Steelhawks	OHL	4	0	1	1	21	0	–	–	–	–
1984–85	Sault Ste. Marie Greyhounds	OHL	44	20	52	72	172	–	6	11	17	60
1985–86	Adirondack Red Wings	AHL	32	12	15	27	152	15	2	3	5	68
1985–86	Detroit Red Wings	NHL	44	8	13	21	186	10	–	–	–	–
1986–87	Adirondack Red Wings	AHL	7	1	4	5	15	–	–	–	–	–
1987–88	Detroit Red Wings	NHL	63	13	11	24	221	–	3	4	7	63
1988–89	Detroit Red Wings	NHL	74	29	33	62	398	16	8	13	21	51
1989–90	Detroit Red Wings	NHL	25	4	2	6	106	16	–	–	–	–
1990–91	Detroit Red Wings	NHL	4	3	0	3	21	–	–	–	–	–
1991–92	Detroit Red Wings	NHL	55	16	23	39	315	–	1	2	3	50
1992–93	Chicago Blackhawks	NHL	63	20	24	44	276	6	1	6	7	28
1993–94	Chicago Blackhawks	NHL	80	14	29	43	292	11	0	3	3	10
1994–95	Chicago Blackhawks	NHL	66	7	10	1	275	7	1	1	2	8
1995–96	Chicago Blackhawks	NHL	78	19	21	40	237	7	0	2	2	23
1996–97	Chicago Blackhawks	NHL	82	9	14	23	326	10	2	1	3	41
1997–98	Chicago Blackhawks	NHL	14	2	1	3	48	6	–	–	–	–
1998–99	Chicago Blackhawks	NHL	78	7	14	21	206	–	–	–	–	–
1999–00	Chicago Blackhawks	NHL	69	4	1	15	114	–	–	–	–	–
2000–01	Chicago Blackhawks	NHL	79	7	12	19	103	–	–	–	–	–
2001–02	Chicago Blackhawks	NHL	61	1	3	4	176	2	0	0	0	0
NHL Totals			935	163	221	384	3300	81	16	32	48	274

Bob Probert is fifth on the NHL's all-time penalty minute list, but he never led the NHL in fights in a single year. The year of his career high 398 penalty minutes in 1987–88, the league's most frequent heavyweight was Bruins goon Jay Miller, who dropped the gloves 34 times that season.

Chapter Four

Stu Grimson

Stu Grimson has been told countless times that he is a walking contradiction. Grimson is a devoutly religious Christian who for 12 years made his living with his fists as one of the NHL's toughest fighters, one so feared he was known around the league as the "Grim Reaper."

He also went from that life of violence and primal supremacy into the peaceful world of academics, finishing his undergraduate degree in economics at the University of Manitoba after he retired from the NHL in 2002 and then earning a degree in law at the University of Memphis.

But Grimson doesn't see those aspects of his life as conflicting. Far from it. The so-called contradiction of being a bruising hockey player and then going on to study law is a non-issue for Grimson. Anyone who knew him during his career as a player would tell you he was a well-spoken, intelligent man who just happened to beat people up for a living. And Grimson says many enforcers are the same way, even though people don't generally perceive NHL tough guys to be scholars-in-waiting.

"I think we're all guilty of doing this to some extent; we see someone play in a certain style or role and we project a whole set of characteristics on them," Grimson says. "When we actually get to know them, we find out they're actually someone quite contrary to those characteristics we kind of hung on them."

As for the apparent contradiction of a religious man using violence to make a living, Grimson doesn't buy that, either. Fighting, he says, has been a part of hockey, in varying degrees of importance, throughout its history. So if fighting is allowed in hockey to the extent that it won't get you kicked out of the game, why should he be denied that aspect of the game just because of his beliefs?

"I often felt it was more an extension of my faith than it was any kind of a contradiction of my faith," he explains. "I would look around the locker room and say, 'If someone has to fill this role, if someone has to stick up for the smaller players and watch the backs of some of the more skilled players, why can't it be a Christian?' Having resolved that internally, it's always a role I filled with a great deal of pride."

And an even greater deal of effectiveness. Throughout his career, Grimson was an imposing figure who scared opponents straight, helped by the fact that at 6'5" and 230 pounds, he was extremely tough to handle when the gloves came off. But it took Grimson a while to realize that his best shot at becoming an NHL hockey player would be to use that brawn to his advantage to intimidate opponents.

Grimson was born in Vancouver, British Columbia, but he spent much of his childhood moving from place to place because his father, an officer with the Royal Canadian Mounted Police, was transferred to various western Canadian towns. Grimson says he was not an aggressive child, though he did get into fights every now and then, like most kids do. When he began playing hockey at age five, and as he moved through the minor ranks, Grimson was actually at a disadvantage because of his size.

"I was always bigger than my peers, so I think size came at the expense of coordination for me," he says. "I needed time to grow into my hands and feet over time."

Grimson eventually found that coordination, making him an interesting prospect by the time

he was ready to move on to the junior ranks with
the Regina Pats of the Western Hockey League in
1982. But at that point, Grimson realized his
hockey skills would only get him so far. In order
to make the jump to that next level, he would
have to find himself a niche that would be val-
ued in the pros.

Grimson slowly began to assert himself as an
enforcer during that first year in Regina, getting
105 penalty minutes in only 48 games in 1982–83.
Although he registered only one assist that season,
the Detroit Red Wings were intrigued enough to
take a chance on him, selecting Grimson in the
10th round of the 1983 NHL draft. The Red Wings
were obviously looking for an enforcer that year,
because they also took Bob Probert in the third
round and Joey Kocur in the fifth, two players
who would eventually combine for 5819 penalty
minutes over their NHL careers.

Grimson, however, never signed with Detroit.
After his third junior season in 1984–85, during
which he racked up 24 goals with 32 assists and
248 penalty minutes, the Calgary Flames picked
him in the seventh round of the 1985 draft. But
rather than turn pro immediately, Grimson
decided to attend the University of Manitoba
and play in the unheralded Canadian Interuni-
versity Athletic Union (CIAU). While studying
economics, Grimson played two seasons for the

Bisons under coach Wayne Fleming, whom he credits with teaching him the many intricacies of the game.

In the summer of 1987, Grimson decided it was time to embark on his professional career. He knew that once he did, however, he would be expected to drop the gloves with some of the toughest men on the planet, and that realization was a daunting one.

Embarking on his professional hockey career should have been the highlight of his life, but Grimson was an emotional wreck as he attempted to come to grips with the difficult journey he was about to undertake.

"I think it was the whole prospect of playing professional hockey, and specifically playing professional hockey in the role I was playing," Grimson says. "That was pretty intimidating to me, and I really wrestled with that a lot. I was just never comfortable in that role at that stage in my life, and I was prepared to walk away from the game altogether."

Instead of doing that, Grimson decided to turn his focus away from himself and all the pressure he created. "I was trying to control things that were out of my control, and at one point I just had to release the reins on those things that were out of my control," he says. "I really came to a place where I recognized that I needed to take myself out of the centre of my life and put God there."

A newfound devotion to Christianity provided Grimson with clarity he never had before, and he was suddenly not only comfortable with being an enforcer, he reveled in it. Grimson was sent to the Salt Lake Golden Eagles of the International Hockey League after being cut by the Calgary Flames in 1987, and over the next two seasons he would gather 665 penalty min- utes in 109 games.

Grimson was called up to the Flames for one game in 1988–89, and he instantly got down to business with his first NHL fight by initiating a scrap with Buffalo Sabres tough guy Kevin Maguire. But it was during another brief call-up in 1989–90 that Grimson secured his reputation as a legitimate NHL heavyweight.

The Flames were visiting their archrivals, the Edmonton Oilers, and their hulking enforcer Dave Brown. Grimson did not waste much time, dropping the gloves with the renowned fighter on his first shift. Grimson got the better of Brown that night, but that wasn't necessarily a good thing. When the Oilers visited Calgary in the back end of a home-and-home series two nights later, Brown got his revenge by pummeling Grimson, fracturing his cheekbone and part of his orbital bone. But that defeat mattered little, because Grimson's reputation was established in those two fights.

"It kind of registered with a lot of decision-makers in the league that I was capable of playing this role at the NHL level based on how things went with Dave Brown on those two nights," he says.

Grimson would only play one more game with Calgary that season before being sent back down to the minors.

Grimson's career took a positive turn when he was picked up on waivers by the Chicago Blackhawks before the following 1990–91 season. Chicago was looking for a guy who could stand up to the bevy of tough guys playing in their division. The Red Wings had Probert, Kocur and Randy McKay, the Minnesota North Stars had Shane Churla and Basil McRae, the St. Louis Blues had Tony Twist and Kelly Chase, and the Toronto Maple Leafs had Wendel Clark and Ken Baumgartner.

"Back then, Chicago was in the Norris Division, and most hockey insiders referred to it as the Chuck Norris Division," Grimson says. "These guys dressed very physical lineups."

Grimson's arrival coincided with that of another legendary tough guy, Mike Peluso, and the Blackhawks won the Norris Division title in 1990–91, while also leading the league in penalty minutes.

Grimson played two more seasons in Chicago before riding the NHL carousel. Between 1993 and 2002, Grimson would play two seasons with the Anaheim Mighty Ducks, two more with the Detroit Red Wings, two with the Hartford Whalers/Carolina Hurricanes franchise, then back to Anaheim for another two seasons, off to Los Angeles for a year with the Kings, and finally landing with the Nashville Predators for the 2001–02 season.

Over that time, Grimson became involved with the NHL Players' Association (NHLPA), first as a team representative and later serving two years as vice-president of the executive committee. Grimson found his work with the NHLPA rewarding, perhaps even more so than his full-time gig as an enforcer, as the business side of the game became more interesting to him.

By the time Grimson arrived in Nashville, he was a veteran of hundreds of NHL fights, and the player had taken his fair share of haymakers. On December 8, 2001, Grimson and the Predators were hosting Georges Laraque and his Edmonton Oilers. The two tough guys squared off, and Laraque, one of the top fighters in the league at the time, landed several heavy lefts to Grimson's head in an entertaining scrap.

The heavy beating Grimson took that night, however, left him with a concussion from which he would never fully recover. As doctors attempted to explain to Grimson the nature of his injury, the Grim Reaper realized he would need to re-evaluate his priorities.

"I had to come to a realization that this wasn't a typical injury for me," Grimson recalls. "It wasn't a shoulder, it wasn't a knee where I could have the surgery and push through it. I had to realize this was a different injury, this was my head. So I had to take some time out and listen to my body. But it was a really educational process for me because athletes are not inclined to think that way when it comes to other parts of your body. But when you're dealing with something like your head, it's clearly a different analysis."

Grimson didn't play the rest of the year. When he still hadn't recovered over the summer, it was becoming questionable whether or not he could be ready in time for the 2002–03 season.

It was only then that Grimson decided not take any unnecessary risks, that he instead would finish the economics degree he started 17 years earlier at the University of Manitoba. Grimson managed to complete the two years remaining on his degree in a single school year. In May 2003, he was in Winnipeg, dressed in a cap and gown, to accept his diploma in front of his four children.

But Grimson knew that a bachelor's degree in economics would not be enough to achieve his new career goals, so he enrolled in law school at the University of Memphis. He had enjoyed his time working for the NHLPA so much that he hoped he could one day get a full-time job with the association. If that didn't work out, he figured, he could become a player agent, allowing him to remain in the game in some capacity.

When he graduated from law school at age 40 in December 2005, Grimson's application to the players association was almost a formality. In March 2006, only three months after Grimson graduated, NHLPA president Ted Saskin announced that Grimson would be joining the association's labor department, handling issues such as player grievances, arbitration cases and league–player discipline. Though most people's eyebrows were raised when the announcement was made, largely because of Grimson's public perception as a nothing more than a goon, he himself saw the move as a natural continuation of the role he filled so admirably over the course of his 12-year NHL playing career.

"I always felt [as an enforcer] I was working for the players, or defending the players in some respect. If you do that for a long enough time, it certainly becomes a part of you persona," Grimson says. "So, perhaps in part, that persona on the ice has evolved into what I'm doing today, in so far as I continue to battle on behalf of the players."

Stu Grimson

Position: Left wing
Date of birth: May 20, 1965
Place of birth: Kamloops, BC

Season	Team	Lge	Regular Season					Playoffs				
			GP	G	A	Pts	PIM	GP	G	A	Pts	PIM
1982–83	Regina Pats	WHL	48	0	1	1	105	5	0	0	0	14
1983–84	Regina Pats	WHL	63	8	8	16	131	21	0	1	1	29
1984–85	Regina Pats	WHL	71	24	32	56	248	8	1	2	3	14
1985–86	U. of Manitoba	CIAU	15	8	5	13	133					
1986–87	U. of Manitoba	CIAU	29	8	8	16	67					
1987–88	Salt Lake Golden Eagles	IHL	37	9	5	14	268	–	–	–	–	–
1988–89	Salt Lake Golden Eagles	IHL	72	9	18	27	397	14	2	3	5	86
1988–89	Calgary Flames	NHL	1	0	0	0	5	–	–	–	–	–
1989–90	Salt Lake Golden Eagles	NHL	62	8	8	16	319	4	0	0	0	8
1989–90	Calgary Flames	NHL	3	0	0	0	17	–	–	–	–	–
1990–91	Chicago Blackhawks	NHL	35	0	1	1	183	5	0	0	0	46
1991–92	Indianapolis Ice	IHL	5	1	1	2	17	–	–	–	–	–
1991–92	Chicago Blackhawks	NHL	54	2	2	4	234	14	0	1	1	10
1992–93	Chicago Blackhawks	NHL	78	1	1	2	193	2	0	0	0	4
1993–94	Anaheim Mighty Ducks	NHL	77	1	5	6	199	–	–	–	–	–
1994–95	Anaheim Mighty Ducks	NHL	31	0	1	1	110	–	–	–	–	–
1994–95	Detroit Red Wings	NHL	11	0	0	0	37	11	1	0	1	26
1995–96	Detroit Red Wings	NHL	56	0	1	1	128	2	0	0	0	0
1996–97	Detroit Red Wings	NHL	1	0	0	0	0	–	–	–	–	–
1996–97	Hartford Whalers	NHL	75	2	2	4	218	–	–	–	–	–
1997–98	Carolina Hurricanes	NHL	82	3	4	7	204	–	–	–	–	–
1998–99	Anaheim Mighty Ducks	NHL	73	3	0	3	158	3	0	0	0	30
1999–00	Anaheim Mighty Ducks	NHL	50	1	2	3	116	–	–	–	–	–
2000–01	Los Angeles Kings	NHL	72	3	2	5	235	5	0	0	0	4
2001–02	Nashville Predators	NHL	30	1	1	2	76	–	–	–	–	–
	NHL Totals		729	17	22	39	2113	42	1	1	2	120

Stu Grimson's average game over his 14 seasons in the NHL went something like this: 0.02 goals, 0.03 assists, 2.89 penalty minutes.

Chapter Five

Ted Lindsay

Ted Lindsay did not have the natural physical tools of his incredible Red Wings linemate Gordie Howe, but the man known as "Scarface" was still one of the nastiest and meanest players in NHL history.

Lindsay stood only 5'8" and weighed 163 pounds, compared to Howe's brawny 6'0", 205-pound frame, and the two of them combined to terrorize the league over a 10-year period where the Detroit Red Wings were the most dominant team in hockey. The two star wingers first played with Sid Abel at center, and later with Alex Delvecchio, to form what was dubbed "The Production Line," a tribute to Detroit's automotive industry. Lindsay made a habit of running people over every chance he got. Over the 10-year lifespan of "The Production Line," Lindsay put together an incredible run of finishing among the league's top 10 in points, goals and penalty minutes in seven straight seasons. The streak was broken only when he missed 21 games in 1954–55. The following year, Lindsay finished sixth in goals, second in penalty minutes and 12th in points.

Several tough guys in league history have had isolated seasons where their scoring prowess matched their physical dominance. Lindsay's run of consistency in that regard may never be matched.

Lindsay's combative nature could be traced back to his youth in Renfrew, Ontario, as the youngest of nine children. He learned the game by playing against his five older brothers and his father, Bert, who was a star goaltender for the Renfrew Millionaires in the early 1900s. In 1940, Lindsay's older brothers all joined the military to fight in World War II, leaving the 15-year-old with no one to practice against. Lindsay went to play for the Holy Name Juveniles for four years before moving on to junior hockey at St. Michael's College, which is where Red Wings head scout Carson Cooper spotted him.

Lindsay made the Red Wings roster as a 19-year-old rookie in 1944–45. Two years later, legendary Red Wings head coach Jack Adams put together "The Production Line," and Detroit went on to win the NHL's regular-season title seven years straight, earning four Stanley Cups along the way.

Lindsay was notorious for the way he forgot all friendships when he was on the ice. Once, while he was playing the Toronto Maple Leafs, Lindsay viciously hounded defenseman Gus Mortson the entire game, despite the fact they were childhood friends, former teammates and even business partners at the time.

"I don't know anybody when a hockey game starts," Lindsay says.

His nickname, "Scarface," is somewhat self-explanatory, and Lindsay says he stopped counting how many stitches he received to his face when he reached 400. However, it was Lindsay who made a career of using a high-stick to keep people honest, a practice that earned him the moniker "Terrible Ted."

Though Lindsay was a key cog in the success of "The Production Line," his combative nature ultimately broke it up. In the mid-1950s, Lindsay spearheaded a movement to get NHL players organized so they could demand better working conditions from the owners, the initial precursor to the NHL Players Association.

"Starting that union was something I believed in very strongly," Lindsay says. "What you had at the time was a dictatorship with the team owners. The owners and managers were too stupid to realize we had brains. They thought we were going to hurt the game, but we just wanted to help ourselves, because the players needed to get together to protect their interests."

Lindsay began gathering the support of the players, and in 1957, he was named president of the first NHL players union. He filed a $3-million lawsuit against NHL owners in an attempt to improve the players' pension benefits and get them a larger share of the television revenue that had started coming in. The court action failed, and the union disbanded shortly thereafter, when several owners pressured their star players to pull out. Coach Adams was furious with the role Lindsay played in getting the union off the ground and traded him to the Chicago Blackhawks as part of a six-player deal in the summer of 1957. That was the end of "The Production Line."

Lindsay was devastated by his exile from the only hockey home he had ever known, and found it difficult to suddenly have to perform for the league doormat Blackhawks.

"I liked playing in Chicago, and I gave them everything I had," Lindsay says, "but I knew in my heart I was a Red Wing. I had that flying wheel tattooed on my forehead."

Lindsay only lasted three seasons in Chicago before deciding in 1960 to hang up his skates and concentrate on his business interests in Detroit.

Four years later, Lindsay was asked to play in an exhibition game of Detroit alumni against the 1964 version of the Red Wings, who were being coached by Lindsay's old centerman Sid Abel. Lindsay agreed, and for old time's sake, Howe (who was still playing for the Red Wings) was recruited to play for the alumni side. "The Production Line" was reunited.

"There must have been about 4000 or 5000 people there to watch the reunion," Lindsay remembers. "We came out and played as if we had never been apart, even taking a 2–0 lead. I think the Red Wings took us too lightly and it took everything they had to beat us. I think the score was 3–2 or 4–3."

Abel, having gotten a first-hand look at the 39-year-old Lindsay's legs, liked what he saw and asked his former winger if he wanted to come back and play another season. Lindsay, after some careful deliberation, decided it was something he had to do.

"I was back in a Red Wings uniform and loving it," he says.

At the 1964–65 Detroit home opener, Lindsay experienced a welcome from the fans that stayed with him forever. It was validation of the years he spent dominating that left wing in Detroit and also redemption for the sour taste of his departure from the team.

"It was very touching, considering the bad circumstances under which I had left the team and that I had been away for four years," Lindsay says. "There was a lot of water under the bridge, but as the ovation built, that water was drying up. As they continued to cheer—it seemed like they kept going for 10 minutes—it made me feel like maybe I did something right. It was very humbling.

"With that kind of pregame buildup, I couldn't let the fans down. I was pretty pumped up when the game started. It felt like old times again. The fans cheering us on, the sights and smells of the arena— and I even got into a fight with Tim Horton, and I drew a 10-minute misconduct."

Lindsay would go on to score 14 goals and 14 assists in 69 games that season, playing primarily on a line with Pit Martin and Bruce MacGregor. But most importantly, he drew 173 penalty minutes, the second-highest total of his career, proving that even a four-year layoff could not take the fight out of Ted Lindsay.

Ted Lindsay

Position: Left wing
Date of birth : July 29, 1925
Place of birth: Renfrew, Ontario

Season	Team	Lge	Regular Season					Playoffs				
			GP	G	A	Pts	PIM	GP	G	A	Pts	PIM
1944–45	Detroit Red Wings	NHL	45	17	6	23	43	14	2	0	2	6
1945–46	Detroit Red Wings	NHL	47	7	10	17	14	5	0	1	1	0
1946–47	Detroit Red Wings	NHL	59	27	15	42	57	5	2	2	4	10
1947–48	Detroit Red Wings	NHL	60	33	19	52	95	10	3	1	4	6
1948–49	Detroit Red Wings	NHL	50	26	28	54	97	11	2		8	31
1949–50	Detroit Red Wings	NHL	69	23	55	78	141	13	4	4	8	16
1950–51	Detroit Red Wings	NHL	67	24	35	59	110	6	0	1	1	8
1951–52	Detroit Red Wings	NHL	70	30	39	69	12	8	5	2	7	8
1952–53	Detroit Red Wings	NHL	70	32	39	71	111	6	4	4	8	6
1953–54	Detroit Red Wings	NHL	70	26	36	62	110	12	4	4	8	14
1954–55	Detroit Red Wings	NHL	49	19	19	38	85	11	7	12	19	12
1955–56	Detroit Red Wings	AHL	67	27	23	50	161	10	6	3	9	22
1956–57	Detroit Red Wings	NHL	70	30	55	85	103	5	2	4	6	8
1957–58	Chicago Blackhawks	NHL	68	15	24	39	110	–	–	–	–	–
1958–59	Chicago Blackhawks	NHL	70	22	36	58	184	6	6	4	6	13
1959–60	Chicago Blackhawks	NHL	68	7	19	26	91	4	4	1	2	0
1964–65	Detroit Red Wings	NHL	69	14	14	28	173	7	7	0	3	34
	NHL Totals		1068	379	472	851	1808	133	133	49	96	194

In addition to being one of the top goal scorers of his era, Ted Lindsay finished in the top 10 in penalty minutes every year between 1947–48 and 1953–54, and also in each of his seasons from 1955–56 to 1964–65. The only time he led the league, however, was in 1958–59 when he spent a career-high 184 minutes in the box with the Chicago Blackhawks.

Chapter Six

Terry O'Reilly

NHL history is rife with players who sported great nicknames, but there may never have been one more appropriate than Terry O'Reilly's "Taz."

The moniker was short for the Tasmanian Devil, a cartoon character who spun around with such force that he would destroy everything in his path. That was exactly how O'Reilly played over the course of his 13-year career with the Boston Bruins, crashing and banging his way all over the ice and, whenever necessary, challenging the opposing team's enforcer.

But O'Reilly had his share of barriers to overcome, not the least of which was a skating style that became a source of frequent mockery from his teammates. "On skates," Bruins legend Bobby Orr once said, "Terry is about as smooth as a stucco bathtub." Good-natured ribbing aside, however, O'Reilly's teammates appreciated what he brought to the game. O'Reilly was skilled at intimidating the other team into mistakes and providing that physical force every good team needs.

To that effect, Orr was very clear as to how valuable O'Reilly really was.

"Give me a team of Terry O'Reillys," Orr said, "and nobody is going to beat me."

O'Reilly's difficulties as a skater, however, made it tough for him to prove himself early in his career. The awkward style could have been a result of the fact that O'Reilly played as a goalie in the Niagara Falls, Ontario, minor hockey system until he was 13 years old. But despite the problem, the Bruins saw fit to draft O'Reilly 14th overall in the first round of the 1971 draft after he compiled 65 points and 151 penalty minutes in his third and final season with the junior Oshawa Generals.

O'Reilly went to his first Bruins training camp later that fall, and immediately impressed management with his confrontational style by taking on veteran defenseman Carol Vadnais in a fight.

"We knew he was a tough junior player and it's always fairly impressive, especially in those days when teams were always on the lookout for tough players, when a rookie would come up and fight one of the tougher veterans," said

Tom Johnson, the Bruins coach at the time. "And he won the fight. But if you beat Terry nine times in a row, you'd have to beat him the 10th, because he'd keep coming after you until he won. And of course, I don't think Terry ever lost nine times in a row."

O'Reilly spent the 1971–72 season fine-tuning his game in the American Hockey League with the Boston Braves, and his future coach Don Cherry remembers his first impression of "Taz" in the minors.

"He wouldn't like me saying this, but he literally could not stand up on his skates," Cherry said. "He'd fall down every time he tried to go fast. I would think, 'What's this guy doing in pro hockey?' And he didn't like you making jokes about his skating. But he must have done something over the summer or something must have clicked, because he was a force the next year. In all my life, I've never seen anyone in sports work as hard as him."

O'Reilly showed the Bruins enough during that year in the minors to earn a one-game call-up at the end of the season on April 2, 1972. He scored a goal against the Maple Leafs that night, laying the groundwork for the love-affair that would follow between the Irishman and the heavily Irish crowds at Boston Garden.

The Bruins went on to win the Stanley Cup in 1972, led by Orr and Phil Esposito, and even though O'Reilly didn't see any action in the play-offs, just being around a championship team gave him the thirst to experience that feeling first hand.

O'Reilly knew that he had a lot to prove going in to the 1972–73 season, despite his sensational NHL debut the previous spring.

"I had a long way to go to prove myself when I first came up to the NHL," O'Reilly says. "I was far from the most polished player around and had to work to improve my skating and balance. I was forced to be a physical player in order to make up for my shortcomings. I wasn't stylish or graceful as a skater, and to stop guys who were, I had to make the most of what I could do."

O'Reilly proved that he could do plenty. He spent his first few seasons playing on checking lines, but in 1976–77, he was teamed with center Peter McNab to form an impressive offensive duo. O'Reilly earned 55 points that year, but in 1977–78 he really blossomed into a star, with 90 points and 211 penalty minutes, becoming the third player in Bruins history to lead the team in both categories. It was also the first time in NHL history a player finished among the top 10 in scoring with more than 200 penalty minutes. O'Reilly's newfound scoring touch was rewarded with his second career all-star game appearance.

"He had that game seven anger in his game every single night," McNab says of his former teammate. "It was always amazing how hard he played the game, every game."

Cherry, who took over as Bruins coach in 1974, was never shy in mentioning that O'Reilly was his favorite player because of the way he made the most of his limited talent. If there was one complaint Cherry had about his agitating winger, it was that he didn't show enough of a killer instinct when he dropped the gloves.

"He was a little too fair," Cherry said. "He would tap guys on the shoulder and ask them if they'd like to fight. I'd say, 'Terry, you're going to get caught one of these times.' Then one time, he tapped Dan Maloney on the shoulder and Danny turned around and broke his nose. So the next time, Terry went after him pretty good."

O'Reilly played with such an edge, with so much passion, that he sometimes went overboard. On October 26, 1977—early in his star season—the Bruins were playing the Minnesota North Stars when O'Reilly was called for a tripping infraction. Enraged, he skated over to confront referee Denis Morel and bumped him before finally throwing his gloves at him to demonstrate his dissatisfaction.

Morel responded by throwing O'Reilly out of the game, and the NHL suspended "Taz" for three more games after that, the only three games he would miss the whole season.

Another time, in the seventh game of the 1982 conference semifinal against the Québec Nordiques, O'Reilly was engaged in a fight when referee Andy Van Hellemond stepped in to put a stop to it. Instead, he received an O'Reilly punch right in the face, forcing the NHL to suspend him for the first 10 games of the following season, since Boston lost the game and was eliminated from the playoffs.

But most of O'Reilly's battles did not result in suspensions; they only inspired teammates and sparked fear in opponents. One great example of this came in the second round of the 1980 playoffs, when Boston went up against the New York Islanders. Although the Bruins lost the series in five games to the eventual Stanley Cup champions, it was not for a lack of effort from O'Reilly. After a relatively calm 2–1 Islander victory in game one, the second game of the series turned into a war, with O'Reilly as its centerpiece.

O'Reilly dropped the gloves with the Islanders' formidable power forward Clark Gillies just over two minutes into the game. To the general surprise of those in attendance, O'Reilly won the fight. The two would square off again with seven seconds left in the first period, with Gillies scoring an early knockdown.

O'Reilly's courage in game two went for naught as the Islanders won 5–4 to take a 2–0 series lead heading to Long Island.

Gillies and O'Reilly squared off twice more in game three, with Gillies landing a big left hand to O'Reilly's nose just as the linesmen were stepping in to stop the second fight. It was just another example of O'Reilly trying his best to overcome his limited skill set with gritty, gutsy play, even though it did not result in a victory for his team.

Later in his career, O'Reilly was plagued with injuries, a result of his signature crash-and-bang style. But even though he suited up for every game with bumps and bruises all over his body, he never changed his approach.

His former teammate Gord Kluzak remembers a time when the Bruins were facing the Philadelphia Flyers in an exhibition game in 1984, O'Reilly's final season. O'Reilly was nursing a bad shoulder, but insisted on suiting up even though the game meant nothing. And that was the real point when it came to O'Reilly: no game ever meant nothing.

Flyers coach Mike Keenan put his enforcers, Darryl Stanley and Glen Cochrane, on the ice at the same time near the end of the game, and Bruins coach Gerry Cheevers countered with the 33-year-old O'Reilly.

"Cochrane outweighed 'Taz' by 30 pounds and was 5 inches taller and lines up next to him on the faceoff," Kluzak recalls. "Typical 'Taz,' here he is with basically one arm, the other was basically useless. Before the puck drops, he absolutely drilled Cochrane with an uppercut, got the first punch in and threw him to the ground and held him. Basically, that's all he could do. But that kind of intensity and refusal to be intimidated, or give anyone an inch was, for a young player seeing that, it was remarkable."

O'Reilly retired in 1985 as the Bruins' all-time leader in penalty minutes with 2095, but more importantly, he was an emotional leader who forced his teammates to give it their all simply because he always did.

"The other guys would see him work in practice and they had to work as hard or they'd look terrible," Cherry said. "He epitomized what it was to be a Boston Bruin at that time."

O'Reilly was honored as such in October of 2002 when the Bruins retired his number 24 alongside those of other greats in Boston's past, from Eddie Shore to Milt Schmidt to Bobby Orr to Phil Esposito to Raymond Bourque.

Though O'Reilly expressed embarrassment at receiving such an honor and having his number hanging next to all those Hall of Fame greats, there is no doubt it was a well-deserved honor for someone who beat the odds to become one of the elite enforcers in league history.

Terry O'Reilly

Position: Right wing
Date of birth: June 7, 1951
Place of birth: Niagara Falls, Ontario

Season	Team	Lge	Regular Season GP	G	A	Pts	PIM	Playoffs GP	G	A	Pts	PIM
1968–69	Oshawa Generals	OHA	46	5	15	20	87					
1969–70	Oshawa Generals	OHA	54	13	36	49	60					
1970–71	Oshawa Generals	OHA	54	23	42	65	151					
1971–72	Boston Braves	AHL	60	9	8	17	134	9	2	2	4	31
1971–72	Boston Bruins	NHL	1	1	0	1	0	–	–	–	–	–
1972–73	Boston Bruins	NHL	72	5	22	27	109	5	0	0	0	2
1973–74	Boston Bruins	NHL	76	11	24	35	94	16	2	5	7	38
1974–75	Boston Bruins	NHL	68	15	20	35	146	3	0	0	0	17
1975–76	Boston Bruins	NHL	80	23	27	50	150	12	3	1	4	25
1976–77	Boston Bruins	NHL	79	14	41	55	147	14	5	6	11	28
1977–78	Boston Bruins	NHL	77	29	61	90	211	15	5	10	15	40
1978–79	Boston Bruins	NHL	80	26	51	77	205	11	0	6	6	25
1979–80	Boston Bruins	NHL	71	19	42	61	265	10	3	6	9	69
1980–81	Boston Bruins	NHL	77	8	35	43	223	3	1	2	3	12
1981–82	Boston Bruins	NHL	70	22	0	52	213	11	5	4	9	56
1982–83	Boston Bruins	AHL	19	6	14	20	10	–	–	–	–	–
1983–84	Boston Bruins	NHL	58	12	18	30	124	3	0	0	0	14
1984–85	Boston Bruins	NHL	63	13	17	30	168	5	1	2	3	9
	NHL Totals	NHL	891	204	402	606	2095	108	25	42	67	335

Terry O'Reilly led the NHL in fights in 1979–80, dropping the gloves 23 times that year on his way to posting a 61-point season and a career-high 265 penalty minutes.

Chapter Seven

Tony Twist

All NHL players have to prepare themselves physically to face the daily rigors of their jobs, and renowned enforcer Tony Twist was no different.

Twist was reputed to be one of the hardest punchers in the league during his 10 seasons with the St. Louis Blues and Québec Nordiques, and once that reputation was set, it became increasingly difficult for him to find a dance partner.

In addition to Twist's size and tremendous strength—he was listed at 6'1", 230 pounds—he took the art of enforcing to a whole new level. Twist never had any delusions about why he was in the NHL. He knew he was there to drop his gloves whenever the situation warranted, and he also knew his chances of staying in the league improved every time he won a fight.

"I never had any skill," Twist says. "My skill was limited to what I did, and I was willing to accept that. That was what I was hired to do, but I prepared for it."

His preparation included scouting his future opponents, and he referred to a library of videos he kept on various tough guys around the league. By the time Twist retired from the NHL in 1999, he had a collection of about 500 tapes.

But the most important preparation ritual Twist underwent was to toughen up his knuckles by punching a concrete floor over and over for about 15 minutes a night while he watched TV. The constant pounding conditioned his fists to recover quickly from a fight, so if Twist pounded on someone in the first period, his knuckles would be ready for another round in the second period.

"It really helped my career, I promise you that," Twist said of the peculiar ritual. "If you fight 33 times in a year, I don't care who you are, if you don't toughen your knuckles up, you're not going to be able to perform."

Twist learned that lesson the hard way as a teenager playing Junior A hockey in Prince George, British Columbia. His bloodlines meant that he was practically born to fight. His grandfather Harry Twist was an accomplished boxer, winning the Canadian welterweight title fighting under the name Harry Rancorn, and his grandmother Ethel was a member of the British Columbia Lacrosse Hall of Fame. His father was a Royal Canadian Mounted Police officer for 32 years, which meant Twist moved around a lot as a child after his birth in Saskatoon, Saskatchewan.

He began playing hockey when he was only four and was quite skilled as a child, but by the time Twist was 16 and ready to start playing for the Junior A Prince George Spruce Kings, he had fallen in love with fighting.

"At 16 years old, I found out I could fight and I enjoyed it," Twist says. "That's just what you had to do to survive, but I really did enjoy it. The league we were playing in was called the Peace Caribou Junior Hockey League, but there was nothing peaceful about it."

Over the next two seasons, Twist would fight in nearly every game, and brawling came to be expected of him.

"The fans in that league came to see one thing, and that was a good fight," Twist says, looking back on those days. "So there were all-out brawls before the game, there were all-out brawls during the game, and there were even a few all-out brawls after the game."

In 1986, Twist went back to his native Saskatoon to play in the Western Hockey League, and in
two seasons with the Blades, he had an unimpres-
sive total of one goal and 16 assists in 119 games.

Given those numbers, no one could blame
Twist for thinking little about his chances of
getting drafted in 1988. In fact, he was weighing scholarship offers from a few colleges that
summer. But even though Twist only managed
17 points in those 119 games with Saskatoon,
his 407 penalty minutes over that period caught
the eye of St. Louis Blues general manager Ron
Caron, and he took the hulking winger in the
ninth round of the 1988 NHL draft. Twist,
stunned at the unexpected development, put
his college plans on hold and attended a few
Blues rookie camps before heading off to his
first NHL training camp in the fall of 1988.

The Blues' incumbent enforcer that year was
Todd Ewen, and there were several others at
camp who weren't shy when it became time for
the rough stuff. Twist decided he wanted a piece
of each of them.

"Going into that first training camp, I figured
I'd just go in there and do what I do, and that's
precisely what I did," Twist says. "The first shift
I had with Todd Ewen, I went after him. The first

shift I had with whoever was out there, I went after him."

Twist's enthusiasm for violence caught the eye of the Blues media, and despite the fact that Twist didn't make the team that year, he was an instant hit in the eyes of St. Louis fans.

Twist played his first professional season in 1988–89 with the Peoria Rivermen of the International Hockey League, spending 312 minutes in the penalty box and earning 33 fighting majors in 67 games. Back at the parent club in St. Louis, Ewen was slapped with a 10-game suspension near the end of the season that would carry over to the next year. Twist knew there was a spot open for him to at least start the 1989–90 campaign in the NHL.

Coach Brian Sutter kept Twist when the Blues broke camp that year, and the next thing he knew, he was climbing the stairs from the visitor's locker room at old Chicago Stadium for his first NHL game against the Blackhawks. Twist took care of his first NHL fight that very same night, squaring off against Chicago's top enforcer, Wayne Van Dorp.

"The first shift I got with him, I went after him and beat him handily. What a great experience, there's no better feeling," Twist says. "You come up against their enforcer, everyone's excited, you beat the [daylights] out of him and every-one's quiet. And I'm just sitting there going, 'I had an impact on 20,000 people, quieted them instantaneously.' It was awesome."

Twist remained in St. Louis for 48 games that season, and even though he only dressed in 28 of them, he managed to send a clear message to the rest of the league.

"After fighting 21 times in 28 games," Twist says, "I think everyone knew what I was there to do."

Twist finished that season and began the next one in Peoria before being traded to the Nor-diques late in the 1990–91 season. Québec was the youngest team in the NHL, featuring bur-geoning stars like Joe Sakic, Mats Sundin and Owen Nolan. Head coach Pierre Pagé had lots of available minutes for Twist when he arrived in town, using him in the Nordiques' final 24 games of the year. Twist was popular not only with Pagé, but also with a lot of fans in Québec who were suffering through a horrible season. Twist's mother was French-Canadian, and by the end of that year he was able to comfortably conduct post-game interviews in French, further endear-ing him to local fans.

Twist spent the next three seasons in Québec, and in February 1992, he had to do something he had never done before: turn down a fight. The Nordiques had reached the month of February without a single win on the road that year before heading to Hartford to face the Whalers.

Québec took a 7–2 lead in the third period, and it looked as though the Nords were assured of finally getting that monkey off their backs. With the game out of reach, Whalers scrapper Ed Kastelic decided he would try to win some points with his coach and teammates by taking on Twist, who by this point had his reputation as the hardest puncher in the league set in stone. Twist had told himself he would never, ever back down from a challenge, but this time the decision was out of his hands.

"He wanted to fight, and Pierre Pagé told me if I got into a fight, he'd kill me," Twist said. "So I didn't fight him that night, but I fought him the next game. That was the only time in my career I ever said no."

Once Twist firmly established himself as a man even the toughest of NHL brawlers didn't want to mess with, his job became significantly easier. The main role of an enforcer is to make opposing players think twice before taking liberties with top players. Twist had become so feared that the simple fact that he was sitting on the bench, licking his chops waiting for someone to step over the line, was enough of a deterrent.

Which is why Twist's career statistics aren't lined with penalty-minute totals as high as most of the league's designated goons. Over his 10-year career, Twist got 1121 penalty minutes in 445 games, an average of only 2.5 minutes per contest.

"I don't think you need to fight every game to do your job," Twist says. "It just came down to the intimidation factor. I was able to perform my job, but that's not to say I didn't want to fight. There were a bunch of times I went out looking for them, but I just wasn't able to get them. But I learned that more could be performed by doing the smart thing."

When Twist did find a partner, his opponent rarely lasted long. Twist's punches were so vicious, those knuckles so toughened, that it rarely took more than one blow to end a fight. If the bout did happen to drag on, it was only because Twist was waiting for an opening through which to land his haymaker.

Twist went back to St. Louis to play for the Blues before the 1994–95 lockout-shortened season, and one of his most frequent opponents over the following four seasons was legendary brawler Bob Probert. Probert, who was playing for the Chicago Blackhawks, represented a huge contrast in fighting style from Twist. The Chicago player preferred to tire his opponents out before unleashing a barrage of lethal rights and lefts.

"He could take a punch, and he could go forever and a day," Twist says. "On the other side of it, I wasn't that guy. I would let you throw four or five, and I'd throw my one, you throw four or five, I throw my one. I don't think there was a National Hockey League fight that ever went more than 40 seconds with me. So there were two different styles there. I wanted to knock your head off and kill you, and he wanted to tire you out then beat the [daylights] out of you."

Following the 1998–99 season, Twist was a free agent, and Blues general manager Larry Pleau made it known he wasn't interested in bringing him back. But Twist had begun negotiating with the Philadelphia Flyers, and he was expecting big things for the future.

"I was in incredible shape, 275 pounds with about four-percent body fat," he says. "There was a good chance I was going to kill someone that year."

But his career was derailed when he got into a nasty motorcycle accident in St. Louis. Driving down the street one day, a car suddenly pulled in front of Twist's motorcycle. Twist hit the car and was thrown from his bike, incredibly landing on his feet about 55 feet away, then skidding on his boots for another 20 feet.

"I skidded like Fred Flintstone," Twist says. "The impact was so hard that I wound up with no jeans on, no underwear, nothing. When I went over the handlebars, they grabbed a little bit of my jeans and ripped them completely off. It broke my three-inch leather belt, and I flipped just once. It was incredible, I don't know how I survived it."

Twist's pelvis was fractured in the front and back, and he suffered a severe left knee injury. The accident spelled the end of Twist's career as an enforcer, but it was the launching point for his life after hockey. Twist settled in the St. Louis area and is now the successful owner of three restaurants that bear the name "Twister's."

Twist's combative nature didn't end with his retirement from the NHL. In 1998, he learned of a character in the popular Spawn comic book named Antonio Twistelli, a mob type who is essentially an enforcer. Twist didn't take kindly to what he calls the unauthorized use of his nickname, and he sued Spawn creator Todd MacFarlane for nearly $25 million, in a case that still dragged on eight years after it began. It's safe to say that has been the longest fight of Twist's life.

Tony Twist

Position: Left wing
Date of birth: May 9, 1968
Place of birth: Sherwood Park, Alberta

Season	Team	Lge	Regular Season					Playoffs				
			GP	G	A	Pts	PIM	GP	G	A	Pts	PIM
1986–87	Saskatoon Blades	WHL	64	0	8	8	181	11	0	1	1	42
1987–88	Saskatoon Blades	WHL	55	1	8	9	226	10	1	1	2	6
1988–89	Peoria Riverman	IHL	67	3	8	11	312	–	–	–	–	–
1989–90	Peoria Riverman	IHL	36	1	5	6	200	5	0	1	1	38
1989–90	St. Louis Blues	NHL	28	0	0	0	124	–	–	–	–	–
1990–91	Peoria Riverman	IHL	38	2	10	12	244	–	–	–	–	–
1990–91	Québec Nordiques	NHL	24	0	0	0	104	–	–	–	–	–
1991–92	Québec Nordiques	NHL	44	0	1	1	164	–	–	–	–	–
1992–93	Québec Nordiques	NHL	34	0	2	2	64	–	–	–	–	–
1993–94	Québec Nordiques	NHL	49	0	4		101	–	–	–	–	–
1994–95	St. Louis Blues	NHL	28	3	0	3	89	1	0	0	0	6
1995–96	St. Louis Blues	NHL	51	3	2	5	100	10	1	1	2	16
1996–97	St. Louis Blues	NHL	64	1	2	3	121	6	0	0	0	0
1997–98	St. Louis Blues	NHL	60	1	1	2	105	–	–	–	–	–
1998–99	St. Louis Blues	NHL	63	2	6	8	149	1	0	0	0	0
	NHL Totals	NHL	445	10	18	28	1121	18	1	1	2	22

Tony Twist truly saved his best for last, notching a career-high eight points in 63 games with the St. Louis Blues in 1998–99. A motorcycle accident that summer nearly claimed his life and almost ended his career. His status as one of the league's hardest and most feared punchers made it so he never passed the 200-penalty-minute mark in his career.

Chapter Eight

Dave Williams

The enforcer role is one that lends itself to neither longevity nor consistency. But Dave "Tiger" Williams was a model of both.

To understand just how remarkable the NHL's all-time leader in penalty minutes was over his 14-year career as one of the league's toughest customers, one need only look at how Williams began his career and how he ended it.

In his first full season with the Toronto Maple Leafs in 1975–76, at the age of 22, Williams had 299 minutes in penalties. By the time he played his final full season for the Los Angeles Kings in 1986–87, Williams was a veteran of well over 100 fights, the cumulative effect of which had left him with a nose as flat as a hockey puck. But Williams, at the age of 33, set a career high with 353 penalty minutes that season, dropping the gloves with the same enthusiasm he displayed as a rookie, if not more.

During the 10 seasons in between, Williams never failed to reach 200 penalty minutes, and he crossed the 300-minute mark five times. Those numbers alone would be enough to cement his place among the great enforcers in hockey history. Williams makes no apologies for his rankling style.

"If I had to do it again, I would probably do it the same way," Williams says of his career. "The thing is, anybody can pretend they can pass the puck, shoot the puck and play on the power play. If you want to find out how great of an all-around player you are, go stand toe-to-toe with some guy 6'3", 230 pounds and then go play the next shift. Not many guys can do that."

But Williams was about much more than just fights. He was a player who could not only knock an opponent to the ice with a stiff jab or an upper-cut that came out of nowhere, but could also fill the score sheet and play on his team's top line.

In his first seven full NHL seasons, Williams scored 159 goals, or nearly 23 per year, while averaging 321 penalty minutes per season.

That combination of skill and toughness has been found in few players over the course of hockey history, especially in the post-expansion era, when designated fighters who contributed little offensively slowly became the norm.

Among the nine tough-guy players ever to pass the 3000-penalty-minute mark, Williams sits second only to Dale Hunter in career scoring with 241 goals, 272 assists and 513 points. Although Hunter was a willing and effective fighter, he was far from being a true enforcer, averaging just over two and a half penalty minutes per game compared with just over four per game for Williams.

Williams' penchant for menacing hockey was identified at an early age. It was his first minor hockey coach in his hometown of Weyburn, Saskatchewan, who decided Williams should be known as "Tiger" because of his fiery temperament and the ferocity he displayed on the ice. Williams was only five years old at the time.

"I've had it all my life," he says of his famous moniker. "It was partly because of my personality and partly because of the way I played on the ice."

Williams played junior hockey for the Swift Current Broncos, where he met his future wife, Brenda. He didn't put up huge offensive numbers in his rookie year of 1971–72. Williams only had 34 points, but he immediately made a physical impression on the league, tallying 278 penalty minutes.

The following season, however, New York Islanders legend Bryan Trottier joined the Broncos, and Williams flourished while playing on his line over the next two seasons, scoring 96 goals with 114 assists for 210 points in 134 games while continuing his rough-and-tumble play. One can only imagine how many points Williams would have had those two final years in junior if he hadn't spent 576 minutes in the penalty box.

Williams' gaudy numbers made him one of the top prospects for the 1974 NHL entry draft, but perceived problems with his skating caused him to drop to the Toronto Maple Leafs' 31st pick overall. Although Williams was accustomed to playing on Swift Current's top line and being an offensive star, he knew he couldn't just waltz into the Maple Leafs training camp and instantly score at will.

"I always scored a lot," Williams says. "When I started in '74, we didn't have many physical guys in Toronto. We had a lot of highly talented ones, and I just started pitching in in that [physical] area. Then one thing leads to another in the NHL, and you get slotted into whatever script they think you should be in."

Williams did not make the Toronto club right out of training camp, but he was effective enough playing for the Central Hockey League's Oklahoma City Blazers that he was called up to the Leafs at midseason and placed on a high-octane line with Darryl Sittler and Ron Ellis.

During that rookie season, Williams was approached by Toronto owner Harold Ballard, who had a policy that all his players had to choose a charity to support.

"If you didn't pick one, he'd pick it for you," says Williams, who considers Ballard one of the nicest men he ever met in hockey. "Mr. Ballard walked into the dressing room and told me that my charity was Special Olympics."

Williams has been a dogged supporter of the movement ever since. He sits on the board of directors of the British Columbia chapter, and was inducted into the provincial Special Olympics Hall of Fame in 2000.

Over his next four seasons with the Maple Leafs, Williams continued taking on all challengers—leading the league in fighting majors in three of those years—while putting up solid offensive numbers. He quickly earned himself a spot in the hearts of the Toronto faithful as one of the team's most popular players, helped in no small part by his charity work and frequent public appearances.

But his policeman role and his 100-percent effort game in and game out also won him the respect of his teammates, who were forced to give everything they had because of the example set by Williams.

Sometimes, however, Williams lost control of his emotions and, in 1976, that lack of control nearly landed him in jail. On October 20, the Leafs were playing the Pittsburgh Penguins when Williams hit Dennis Owchar in the head with his stick. The resulting cut on Owchar's head required 46 stitches to close, and the province of Ontario filed assault charges against Williams. He was acquitted. Another time, in his only career fight against Flyers tough guy Dave "The Hammer" Schultz, Williams became so enraged he bit Schultz in the face.

"You consent to assault when you lace up your skates," Williams once said. "It's what hockey is all about."

The ultimate proof that Williams feared absolutely no one came in 1980, when he took on fearsome Edmonton Oilers tough guy Dave Semenko, all 6'3", 215 pounds of him. Playing in Edmonton, Williams and Semenko clashed behind the Maple Leafs net and exchanged a few punches before Williams, to the utter shock of Oilers fans, caught Semenko square in the jaw with a huge right hand. Semenko fell to one knee before quickly rising, swinging away, but Williams knew he had his opponent exactly where he wanted him. Williams hit him with a barrage of punches, culminating with a massive uppercut that sent Semenko sprawling to the ice for good with blood oozing from his lip and nose.

When asked after the game how it felt taking on Semenko, Williams simply replied: "He's a bum."

That fight became legendary in NHL dressing rooms, but despite Williams' display of courage, his days as a member of the Maple Leafs were numbered. Shortly after the Semenko scrap, Maple Leafs general manager Punch Imlach sent Williams to the lowly Vancouver Canucks along with Jerry Butler in exchange for Rick Vaive and Bill Derlago. Williams was not particularly pleased with the development, but he didn't carry that sentiment westward to Vancouver, where he was determined to win over his new teammates and fans.

Three days after the trade, the Flyers came to Vancouver to take on the Canucks and Williams went on a free-for-all. He took on Flyers tough guy Paul Holmgren, then Mel Bridgman, and before long the two teams were engaged in a bench-clearing brawl that resulted in 344 total penalty minutes. Canucks fans loved it.

"He was the new version of Eddie Shack," says Canucks teammate Kevin McCarthy, referring to the former Maple Leafs great. "They were entertainers. Tiger did everything for a reason, not just something that popped up. A lot of the stuff he did was premeditated and thought out for a reason, whether it was to get the other team upset or something else." ·

The ultimate example of McCarthy's words occurred later during that 1979–80 season. In his first game back at Toronto's Maple Leaf Gardens Williams scored the winning goal for the Canucks, but it was his celebration afterward that became his trademark. Williams mounted his stick like a horse and rode it down the ice, taunting the Maple Leafs players, their fans and, most importantly, Imlach watching from his general manager's box high above the ice. That image became a defining one for Williams, but even though he often had wild celebrations for his important goals, he says that was the only time he used that particular one.

"Everybody, a lot of people, think that this happened hundreds and hundreds of times," Williams says. "But I only did it once. That's the greatest thing about it. When you do something, and it is unique, it sticks in the memory for a long time."

Williams' arrival in Vancouver gave the Canucks a much-needed shot in the arm as they rode his energy into the 1980 playoffs. Vancouver's first-round opponent was the Buffalo Sabres, coached by the legendary Scotty Bowman.

The high-powered Sabres jumped to a 2–0 lead in the best-of-five series before heading west for game three. Williams was determined to lead his new team back into the series, so he agitated the Sabres to the point of becoming a distraction. Williams was at the center of a particularly spirited showdown in front of the Sabres bench when, allegedly, he hit Bowman in the head with his stick. The referee didn't call a penalty, and Williams has always denied he ever did it, but Bowman is steadfast.

"It was a real two-hander," he said. "He whacked me, and nobody saw it."

Well, not exactly. Although Williams played on in the game and led the Canucks to a 5–4 win, an NHL supervisor watching from the press box said he saw the elusive whack, and Williams was suspended for Vancouver's 3–1 loss in game four.

The 1980–81 season was the best of Williams' career. He led the Canucks with a career-high 35 goals and was on top of the league in penalty minutes, with 343 in 77 games. He was also the first Canuck ever to be voted to start the All-Star Game that year, and Williams remained true to form by accidentally knocking Islanders great Mike Bossy to the ice in a huge collision.

But it was the following season that was the most remarkable of Williams' tenure in Vancouver, and not only because he passed Bryan Watson as the NHL's all-time penalty-minute leader. The 1981–82 Canucks finished with a mediocre 77 points, losing three more games than they won. Of course, no one was expecting much out of them in the playoffs.

But in round one, Williams scored an overtime goal in game two and the series-clincher in game three as Vancouver swept the Calgary Flames for the Canucks' first playoff series win in franchise history. The Canucks then easily disposed of the Los Angeles Kings and Chicago Blackhawks—who had pulled off major upsets to clear Vancouver's path—in five games each to reach the Stanley Cup final against the powerhouse New York Islanders. But that's when Vancouver's Cinderella run ended, with the Islanders posting an easy four-game sweep.

Williams finished that playoff run with 10 points and 116 penalty minutes in 17 games, playing his role to perfection, but his offensive production waned over the next two seasons until the summer of 1984, when he was traded to the Detroit Red Wings. Williams didn't last long in Motor City as the Red Wings essentially gave up on him after he scored only 3 goals in 55 games, sending him down to play in the minors before shipping him off to the Los Angeles Kings.

But once he was back on the West Coast, Williams proved he had a lot of good hockey left in his 30-year-old legs and fists, scoring in his first game with the Kings and finishing the 1984–85 season with 7 points and 43 penalty minutes in his final 12 games. The Kings weren't counting on Williams to play much the following year, but he quickly forced them to have a change of heart.

"We were planning on playing him some, but he came out of camp as our best left wing," Kings coach Pat Quinn said early in the 1985–86 season. "People have a way of underestimating his skills. The guy is a competitive marvel. In his own way, he knows what he can do. L.A. seems to be a tough town for the guys to keep their minds on their business, but Tiger doesn't have any problem."

Williams finished the season as the Kings' fourth-leading scorer with 20 goals and 29 assists while leading the team with 320 penalty minutes, but he didn't want to hear anyone say he was making a comeback.

"There's no such word," he said. "There are a lot of stupid people in the league who thought I was finished. But I'm not one of the stupid ones."

Williams had another productive year for Los Angeles in 1986–87, but the following year he was released by the Kings only two games into the season and picked up by the Hartford Whalers, where he played another 26 games before calling it a career at the age of 34.

But the end of his playing career was only the beginning of the second phase of Williams' life as a successful businessman and champion of his favorite causes. In addition to his work with the British Columbia Special Olympics, Williams also took up a campaign to save street hockey from being legislated out of Canadian culture when municipal bylaws banning the traditional game began sprouting up.

Williams also became a regular in old-timers charity games, once playing on the same line as former foes Dave Semenko and Dave "The Hammer" Schultz, and he took his responsibility as an entertainer just as seriously in those games as he did during his 14-year NHL career.

Dave "Tiger" Williams

Position: Forward
Date of birth: February 3, 1954
Place of birth: Weyburn, Saskatchewan

Season	Team	Lge	Regular Season					Playoffs				
			GP	G	A	Pts	PIM	GP	G	A	Pts	PIM
1971–72	Swift Current Broncos	WCHL	68	12	22	34	278					
1972–73	Swift Current Broncos	WCHL	68	44	58	102	266					
1973–74	Swift Current Broncos	WCHL	66	52	56	108	310					
1974–75	Oklahoma City Blazers	CHL	39	16	11	27	202	–				
1974–75	Toronto Maple Leafs	NHL	42	10	19	29	187	7	1	3	4	25
1975–76	Toronto Maple Leafs	NHL	78	21	19	40	299	10	0	0	0	75
1976–77	Toronto Maple Leafs	NHL	77	18	25	43	338	9	3	6	9	29
1977–78	Toronto Maple Leafs	NHL	78	19	31	50	351	12	1	2	3	63
1978–79	Toronto Maple Leafs	NHL	77	19	20	39	298	6	0	0	0	48
1979–80	Toronto Maple Leafs	NHL	55	22	18	40	197	–	–	–	–	–
1979–80	Vancouver Canucks	NHL	23	8	5	13	81	3	0	0	0	20
1980–81	Vancouver Canucks	NHL	77	35	27	62	343	3	0	0	0	20
1981–82	Vancouver Canucks	NHL	77	17	21	38	341	17	3	7	10	116
1982–83	Vancouver Canucks	NHL	68	8	13	21	265	4	0	3	3	12
1983–84	Vancouver Canucks	NHL	67	15	16	31	294	4	1	0	1	13
1984–85	Adirondack Red Wings	AHL	8	5	2	7	4	–	–	–	–	–
1984–85	Detroit Red Wiings	NHL	55	3	8	11	158	–	–	–	–	–
1984–85	Los Angeles Kings	NHL	12	4	3	7	43	3	0	0	0	4
1985–86	Los Angeles Kings	NHL	72	20	29	9	320	–	–	–	–	–
1986–87	Los Angeles Kings	NHL	76	16	18	34	358	5	3	2	5	30
1987–88	Los Angeles Kings	NHL	2	0	0	0	6	–	–	–	–	–
1987–88	Hartford Whalers	NHL	26	6	0	6	87	–	–	–	–	–
	NHL Totals		962	241	272	513	3966	83	12	23	35	455

Dave Williams had his first 300-penalty-minute season with the Toronto Maple Leafs in 1976–77 (he finished with 299 minutes in the box in 1975–76), while his final one came a full 10 years later with the Los Angeles Kings in 1986–87 when he was 33 years old. He passed the milestone six times over his career, leaving him as the NHL's all-time penalty-minute king.

Chapter Nine

Gordie Howe

Gordie Howe's incredible professional hockey career, in which he played a staggering 32 seasons in two leagues, is a feat of physical endurance that, in and of itself, makes him one of the toughest men ever to play the game.

But that record of longevity is made all the more unbelievable because of the way Howe played the game over those 32 seasons, with his vicious retribution for anyone who happened to get in his way.

Howe often liked to call his stick "the great equalizer" because of the way he mastered cutting guys who got under his skin, and his elbows became notorious for delivering punishing blows that served as grim warnings for opposing defenders.

Howe's son Marty, who lined up alongside his dad for the Houston Aeros of the World Hockey

Association, once described the formula Howe used to determine the method of his ruthlessness.

"It didn't matter whether he knew you or not, he would still cut you," Marty said. "You didn't make him look stupid. If you tried to make him look stupid, you would get hit with a stick real quick. He didn't like getting hooked from behind in the ribs. He had busted his ribs so many times that that used to aggravate him. If you did that, you got the stick or the elbow, depending on how close you were. In front of the net, defensemen like to hold [a forward's] stick because then you know where they are without looking. If you did that, he would start to skate away like most people do, but then the stick would come back and he would try to take your chin off."

Montréal Canadiens enforcer John Ferguson, who had the unenviable task of shadowing Howe, called him the toughest player he ever had to face.

"He was tough and mean," said Ferguson, himself one of the all-time meanest. "He had guys frightened to death."

Howe, born in Floral, Saskatchewan (a farming town near Saskatoon), was the fourth of nine children. He grew up in a harsh time as Canada worked to emerge from the Great Depression.

Howe was a passionate hockey fan as a child, mailing in labels of Bee Hive corn syrup to get pictures of his NHL heroes, and he desperately wanted to play the game despite lacking the means to do so. The first time he skated at the age of five on the pond behind the Howe family home, he only had one skate, because his sister had the other. When he finally got to try out for his first organized hockey team at age 12, a distraught Howe was sent home because he didn't have the right equipment.

"The only equipment I had was skates and a stick," Howe says. "I took magazincs and mail-order catalogues, stuck them in my socks, and had shin pads. I tied them together with rubber bands made from inner tubes."

Howe was taught by his father, Albert, to always stick up for himself. Albert gave his son a demonstration one time in a Saskatoon pool hall. Howe's father was trying to play pool, but a man kept tapping his hand whenever he set up to take a shot. The elder Howe dropped the guy with a knockout punch.

Howe's fearsome aura took shape in 1946, right at the start of his glorious career when he was 18 years old. He was already an imposing sight, standing 6 feet tall and weighing a solid 205 pounds. To get an idea of how big Howe actually was, it's useful to compare him to other players of that era.

Montréal Canadiens great Maurice "the Rocket" Richard, one of the league's nastier players, was 5'10", 180 pounds. Boston Bruins sniper Milt Schmidt was just as tall as Howe, but 20 pounds lighter. And the Chicago Blackhawks brother tandem of Max and Doug Bentley were listed at 158 and 145 pounds, respectively, and neither of them reached 5'10".

Howe was so advanced in his physical development that he attended the New York Rangers training camp in Winnipeg in 1943, when he was only 15 years old. Howe eventually left camp, not because he couldn't handle it physically, but because he was homesick. Detroit Red Wings western scout Fred Pinckney identified Howe as a can't-miss prospect and signed him to a contract in 1944, a year after the New York Rangers first got a look at him.

After a year of junior hockey in Galt, Ontario, Howe was sent to Nebraska to play for the Omaha Knights of the United States Hockey League in 1945. His coach in Omaha was Tommy Ivan, who would work with Howe again in Detroit from 1947 to 1954. Ivan decided he would ease his young star in slowly, but Howe quickly proved he didn't need to be treated with kid gloves just because he was 17.

"One time, one of our teammates was having a real problem [with another player], and I jumped on the ice and took on the man that was fighting him," Howe says. "Those days, there were no helmets and I was kind of a crazy man anyway, so I bumped his head on the ice. That was the end of the fight."

As Howe skated off the ice, Ivan asked his rookie what had possessed him to do something so rash. "What's the matter? Don't you like him?" Ivan asked Howe.

"I don't like anyone out here," was Howe's reply. That was all Ivan needed to hear, and Howe's ice time quickly increased. He would finish the season with 22 goals in 51 games, and the majority of those were scored after that coming-of-age moment.

Howe's arrival with the Detroit Red Wings was hotly anticipated as a result of his tremendous finish in Omaha, and on October 16, 1946, he would begin a journey through professional hockey that would span 34 years. (Howe had a two-year hiatus during the 1971–72 and 1972–73 seasons, before moving on to the WHA.) Howe was in the starting lineup that night at the Olympia Stadium in Detroit against the Toronto Maple Leafs, and he immediately displayed the two major characteristics of his game that would define his hockey career.

The first—a deft scoring touch—was shown at 13:39 of the second period when Howe buried a shot off the rush, scoring the first of his 801 career NHL goals. Howe's second defining characteristic—a nasty temper—also came out in the second period when he got into a fight with Leafs winger Gaye Stewart and later threw Toronto's star center, Syl Apps, to the ice in a heap.

Howe's rookie season fizzled after that momentous debut, but he learned a lot about how to play the game with an edge by living with teammate "Terrible" Ted Lindsay. The pair would go on to form one of the most productive and disruptive tandems in NHL history.

After that season, Howe's reputation as a tough customer grew with every game he played with the Red Wings, but it climaxed on February 1, 1959, in New York's Madison Square Garden. By that point, Howe was the best player in the league, owner of four Hart Trophies and five NHL scoring titles—including four in a row from 1951 to 1954. But that didn't mean his ornery temperament had faded.

That night in New York, Howe and the rest of the Red Wings were roughing up young Rangers winger Eddie Shack, and at one point Howe cut him for three stitches. Rangers tough guy Lou Fontinato skated over to Howe to warn him there would be consequences if he touched Shack again. Of course, Howe was never intimidated by anyone, and moments later he ran at Shack behind the net. Fontinato quickly arrived on the scene, the gloves were dropped, and he and Howe embarked on a fight that many people believe to be the best in NHL history.

Fontinato probably isn't one of those people. Howe pasted him with a barrage of punches that left Fontinato's face in shambles, breaking his nose to the point that it was bent at a 45-degree angle.

"Howe began smashing him with lefts and rights and then fired an uppercut that smashed Lou's nose," says Art Skov, one of the officials that night. "I just stood back and said, 'No way I'm going to break up this one.' Big George Hayes was the other linesman in the game and he told me to stay out of it. Howe cleaned Fontinato like you've never seen."

From that moment onward, everyone in the NHL knew that if there was one player not to be messed with, it was Gordie Howe.

Howe didn't fight as often later in his career, largely because no one would agree to it, but also because he was a master at picking the right opportunities. If he felt he was wronged in any way, Howe would bide his time until the moment was perfect and eventually get his revenge. A classic example of Howe's trait involved Chicago Blackhawks star Stan Mikita, early in Mikita's career.

Mikita hit Howe with a high stick during a game, and his teammates on the bench warned the young player to be on the lookout, because Howe was sure to come after him. The game continued. Howe never so much as laid a finger on Mikita, who by then believed his teammates were making too much of Howe's reputation. A few games later, with Mikita having long forgotten the incident, Howe skated by and cut him with his stick before nailing him with an elbow. The lesson given to Mikita that night was one all rookies had to endure throughout Howe's career. The first time Howe would face a player, he always did something to make it clear that he was in charge and wasn't to be touched.

"He tested every rookie," former St. Louis Blues player Bob Plager says. "He straightened them out and he got plenty of room."

Howe finished his career with 801 NHL and 174 WHA goals for a total of 975 goals in 32 professional seasons, a mark that withstood even Wayne Gretzky's onslaught on the NHL record books (Gretzky scored 940 career goals in the NHL and WHA combined).

Much of Howe's scoring prowess came from the respect he commanded from his opponents, who were so frightened of incurring his wrath that they rarely went near him.

Gordie Howe

Position: Right wing
Date of birth : March 31, 1928
Place of birth: Floral, Saskatchewan

Season	Team	Lge	Regular Season					Playoffs				
			GP	G	A	Pts	PIM	GP	G	A	Pts	PIM
1945–46	Omaha Knights	USHL	51	22	26	48	53	6	2	1	3	15
1946–47	Detroit Red Wings	WHL	58	7	15	22	52	5	0	0	0	18
1947–48	Detroit Red Wings	WHL	60	16	28	44	63	10	1	1	2	11
1948–49	Detroit Red Wings	CIAU	40	12	25	37	57	11	8	3	11	19
1949–50	Detroit Red Wings	CIAU	70	35	33	68	69	1	0	0	0	7
1950–51	Detroit Red Wings	IHL	70	43	43	86	74	6	4	3	7	4
1951–52	Detroit Red Wings	IHL	70	47	39	86	78	8	2	5	7	2
1952–53	Detroit Red Wings	NHL	70	49	46	95	57	6	2	5	7	2
1953–54	Detroit Red Wings	NHL	70	33	48	81	109	12	4	5	9	31
1954–55	Detroit Red Wings	NHL	64	29	33	62	68	11	9	11	20	24
1955–56	Detroit Red Wings	NHL	70	38	41	79	100	10	3	9	12	8
1956–57	Detroit Red Wings	IHL	70	44	45	89	72	5	2	5	7	6
1957–58	Detroit Red Wings	NHL	64	33	44	77	40	4	1	1	2	0
1958–59	Detroit Red Wings	NHL	70	32	46	78	57	–	–	–	–	–
1959–60	Detroit Red Wings	NHL	70	28	45	73	46	6	1	5	6	4
1960–61	Detroit Red Wings	NHL	64	23	49	72	30	11	4	11	15	10
1961–62	Detroit Red Wings	NHL	70	33	44	77	54	–	–	–	–	–
1962–63	Detroit Red Wings	NHL	70	38	48	86	100	11	7	9	16	22
1963–64	Detroit Red Wings	NHL	69	26	47	73	70	14	9	10	19	16
1964–65	Detroit Red Wings	NHL	70	29	47	76	104	7	4	2	6	20
1965–66	Detroit Red Wings	NHL	70	29	46	75	83	12	4	6	10	12
1966–67	Detroit Red Wings	NHL	69	25	40	65	53	–	–	–	–	–
1967–68	Detroit Red Wings	NHL	74	39	43	82	53	–	–	–	–	–
1968–69	Detroit Red Wings	NHL	76	44	59	103	58	–	–	–	–	–
1969–70	Detroit Red Wings	NHL	76	31	40	71	58	4	0	0	2	2
1970–71	Detroit Red Wings	NHL	63	23	29	52	38	–	–	–	–	–
1971–72	Did Not Play	Ind	Statistics Unavailable									
1972–73	Did Not Play	Ind										
1973–74	Houston Aeros	WHA	70	31	69	100	46	13	3	14	17	34
1974–75	Houston Aeros	WHA	75	34	65	99	84	13	8	12	20	20
1975–76	Houston Aeros	WHA	78	32	70	102	76	17	4	8	12	31
1976–77	Houston Aeros	WHA	62	24	44	68	57	11	5	3	8	11

Season	Team	Lge	Regular Season					Playoffs				
			GP	G	A	Pts	PIM	GP	G	A	Pts	PIM
1977–78	New England Whalers	WHA	76	34	62	96	85	14	5	5	10	15
1978–79	New England Whalers	WHA	58	19	24	43	51	10	3	1	4	4
1979–80	Hartford Whalers	NHL	80	15	26	41	42	3	1	1	2	2
1997–98	Detroit Vipers	IHL	1	0	0	0	0	–	–	–	–	–
	WHA Totals		419	174	334	508	399	78	28	43	71	115
	NHL Totals		1767	801	1049	1850	1685	157	68	92	160	220

Don't let Gordie Howe's relatively low penalty-minute totals fool you into thinking he was Mr. Nice Guy on the ice. His lack of time in the box can be explained two ways. First, few players in the NHL dared fight Howe, because they knew they would be left bloodied at the end. Secondly, and perhaps most importantly, Howe was a master at saving his retaliation for when the referee wasn't looking, meaning most of his vicious infractions went unpenalized.

Chapter Ten

Dave Schultz

The National Hockey League of the 1970s was dominated by two teams that could not have been more different.

The Montréal Canadiens won four straight Stanley Cups to close out the decade, the first of those in 1976, when they swept two-time defending champions the Philadelphia Flyers in the final. The Canadiens of that era were a highly skilled, finesse team led by the likes of Guy Lafleur, Pete Mahovolich, Steve Shutt, Yvan Cournoyer and Jacques Lemaire up front, as well as the "Big Three" of Guy Lapointe, Larry Robinson and Serge Savard on the blue line.

The Flyers were on the other end of the hockey spectrum. They earned the nickname "Broad Street Bullies" because of the sheer intimidation power of their enforcers, an effective style that earned the Flyers back-to-back Stanley Cups in

1974 and 1975 only a short time after the team entered the NHL in the 1967 expansion year. The Flyers counted on the likes of Andre "Moose" Dupont, Bob "Hound Dog" Kelly, Don "Big Bird" Saleski and Gary Dornhoefer to "bully" their opponents into submission.

But no one epitomized the true spirit of the "Broad Street Bullies" era more than Dave "The Hammer" Schultz. Although he was the most feared and revered enforcer of those great Flyer teams, and perhaps in NHL history, Schultz came to the realization that he could make a decent living with his fists relatively late in life. As a boy growing up in rural Saskatchewan, Schultz did not have the type of childhood most people associate with someone who turned into such a terror on the ice.

"I've never had a street fight in my life," Schultz said. "I used to get my brother or my buddy's brother if anyone wanted to do anything with me. So I was a pretty mild, meek, quiet guy."

Schultz began playing hockey with his older brother on the family farm, and his on-ice persona was defined more by his penchant for scoring goals than for knocking guys out. In his two seasons of junior hockey with the Swift Current Broncos, Schultz scored 51 goals with 50 assists in 92 games. Though he also accumulated more than 200 penalty minutes in those two seasons, Schultz says those were earned by his aggressive play and not necessarily because he dropped his gloves. He got into only two fights his whole junior career, and in one of them he didn't even have time to drop his gloves before getting dropped with a shot to the forehead.

"I was nowhere close to being a tough guy, I was just a little scrappy," Schultz said. "There used to be brawls in junior, and I'd be glad I was on the bench."

Schultz's scoring touch and chippy style of play were intriguing enough for the Flyers to select him in the fifth round of the 1969 entry draft. That same year, the Flyers also selected Bob Clarke (future captain of the "Broad Street Bullies") in the second round and "Big Bird" Saleski in the sixth round, while "Moose" Dupont was a first-round pick by the New York Rangers.

Schultz went to Flyers training camp in 1969 and he eventually was dispatched to the Salem Valley Rebels for some seasoning. The Rebels played in the rough-and-tumble Eastern Hockey League, the same league that served as the inspiration for the cult classic 1977 movie *Slap Shot*. In Schultz's first game with Salem that year, he got into two fights, which would open his eyes to a whole new side of hockey, one he could excel at. "That changed my whole career," he said.

Schultz would finish the 1969–70 season with 32 goals, 37 assists and 356 penalty minutes in 67 games, earning him the nickname "Sergeant" Schultz. That season was the foundation for his future as the NHL's pre-eminent enforcer.

"We had some big guys on our team, but no one who seemed to want to fight," Schultz recounted. "So I quickly became that guy. The fans started cheering for it and wanting it. I kind of enjoyed that. I didn't enjoy the fighting, but I enjoyed the rewards. So I just concentrated on that, but I still wanted to play hockey."

The following year, Schultz was promoted to the Flyers' top minor-league team, the Québec Aces of the American Hockey League. Schultz led the AHL with 382 penalty minutes in 1970–71, nearly double the total of the next-highest player on that list. Schultz again led the AHL with 392 penalty minutes playing for the Richmond Robins a year later.

It was during his time in the AHL that Schultz saw first-hand how he could become a fan favorite with his fists. One time, when Schultz was in Providence, Rhode Island, to play the Reds, which featured his future Flyers teammate "Moose" Dupont, the game was promoted as a major fighting event.

"The newspaper in Providence put pictures on the front page of me and Dupont. I mean, that's how they promoted the game, it was going to be Schultz versus Dupont," Schultz said. "There was always that build-up in the minor leagues, and even in the NHL."

Schultz attended his fourth Flyers training camp in 1972 and this time, he made the team. About 10 games into his first season, the Flyers were to host the Chicago Blackhawks and their tough-as-nails defenseman, Keith Magnuson. Schultz nailed Magnuson with a hard hit behind the net during that game, and he knew there would be retribution. Right after the ensuing faceoff, Magnuson made a beeline for Schultz and the two squared off. Flyers fans loved it.

"The Flyers themselves knew what I had been doing for three years in the minor leagues," Schultz said, "but the fans didn't."

With that fight, Schultz, and by extension the Flyers, began building an identity. Schultz's persona was established early that season by Philadelphia Bulletin reporter Jack Chevalier. After a game in which Schultz had a particularly dominant fight, Chevalier was interviewing

Schultz about it when he said, "Boy, did you ever hammer that guy!"

The name stuck, and Schultz was known as "The Hammer" from that point on.

Schultz finished his rookie season with 9 goals and 12 assists, but he led the NHL with 19 fighting majors that season and 259 penalty minutes. The Flyers made the playoffs and won their first series in franchise history, downing the Minnesota North Stars in six games before losing in five to the Canadiens in the second round. Schultz managed to rack up 51 penalty minutes in only 11 playoff games.

Over the following three seasons, Schultz established himself as by far the most feared fighter in the league.

"I visualized what I was going to do, but I also had a certain little technique for grabbing the guy," Schultz said, trying to explain his effectiveness as a fighter. "Sometimes, I'd have to take a few shots to the face to just get me going. But the biggest thing for me was to make sure the fight lasted a while. Once I grabbed on and started swinging, I wasn't going to stop."

Schultz had the best season of his career in 1973–74, scoring 20 goals with 16 assists in 73 games, and again leading the league in penalty minutes with 348. But it was his performance in that year's playoffs that was most eye-catching.

The Flyers swept the Atlanta Flames in the first round, beat the New York Rangers in seven in the second round, and finally took care of the hated Boston Bruins in the Stanley Cup final with a six-game victory. Along the way, Schultz racked up an astonishing 139 penalty minutes in 17 playoff games—an average of more than eight minutes per game—to go with 2 goals and 4 assists.

Though the Flyers' use of intimidation was a big part of that championship season, the tactic was used only because the threat of retribution allowed Philadelphia's star players, such as Bob Clarke and Rick MacLeish, to shine without having to worry about cheap shots.

"We weren't very well liked, and a lot of people were very critical. A lot of times we didn't even start it, but we certainly had a reputation to live up to. The newspapers would be telling people to hide the women and children because the animals were coming," Schultz said. "The 'Broad Street Bullies' themselves, with our team having a nickname, we fed off of that, I suppose. But the key was that we had a great team."

The Flyers' greatness was displayed again in 1974–75 with their second-straight Stanley Cup championship, but it was also the year Schultz put his stamp on NHL history. He piled up a ridiculous total of 472 penalty minutes in 76 regular-season games, a league record that has not come close to being broken. He racked up that number with 61 minor penalties, 26 fighting majors and 22 misconducts. In a single game early that season, Schultz was assessed a total of 58 minutes worth of penalties with two minors, two fighting majors, one 10-minute misconduct and a 34-minute game misconduct.

"He knew his job as well as anyone in the league," said Schultz's former Flyers teammate, Bill Clement. "He would seek out the other team's tough guy at the start of the game and establish that he was the king of the hill. When he wanted to be in the ring, he was the best."

However, Schultz didn't always want to be in the ring, as it were, even though his prowess as a fighter brought him great notoriety with fans all over the league. He said that when he looked ahead in the schedule to mentally prepare himself for who he would have to fight on a given night, it wasn't always pleasant.

"There were times when I didn't want to look at the schedule to know we were going into, say, Boston in two weeks. I didn't want to know that, I didn't want to have to think about it," Schultz said. "If a team didn't really have a guy that was going to stand up to me, it just made it so that it would be an easier game for me. I could actually concentrate on playing a bit of hockey."

Boston was a difficult place for Schultz to play, seeing as the Bruins matched up pretty well with the Flyers in terms of toughness with guys such as Wayne Cashman and, most particularly, Terry O'Reilly. Schultz always said O'Reilly was the toughest guy he ever had to fight.

"I know I fought him at least eight times," Schultz said of his opponent. "He was the heart and soul of the Boston Bruins, and he was a tough guy. He fought every chance he got, he was always ready."

Another great fighter of that era was Dave "Tiger" Williams, the NHL's all-time leader in penalty minutes. Schultz admitted Williams was one guy he tried to avoid.

"I didn't like the way he fought, he liked to fight in close," Schultz said. "But I don't think he came looking for me too often, either."

The one time Schultz did fight Williams came in game six of the second round of the 1976 play-offs between the Flyers and Williams' Toronto Maple Leafs, and that altercation landed Schultz in the NHL record book once more. Williams was playing his role and trying to engage Bob Clarke in a confrontation when Schultz came in and dropped the gloves. During that fight, Schultz claimed Williams bit him in the cheek, but it was Schultz who took the brunt of the referee's wrath that night. Over the course of the game, Schultz was handed one minor penalty, two majors, one 10-minute misconduct and two game misconducts for a total of 42 penalty minutes, an NHL playoff record that stands to this day.

After the game, Flyers general manager Keith Allen asked Schultz to see league commissioner Clarence Campbell, who was waiting for him in another room.

"Tell him what happened," Allen said to Schultz.

"Well, he kneed me, he head-butted me and then he bit me," Schultz told Campbell.

The venerable league commissioner thought about what Schultz told him for a moment, then responded.

"What were you doing there, anyway?" Campbell asked.

That was the end of that.

Of course, that night was not the first time Schultz had to explain his actions to the commissioner. In fact, he had to speak to Campbell so frequently that Schultz had his personal phone number. Despite the frequent talks, Campbell knew very well that the antics of Schultz and Williams and O'Reilly were a huge selling point for the league, and he rarely, if ever, handed down any major sanctions on the league's tough guys.

"Whenever there was an altercation or something, Keith Allen would come to me and say, 'Dave, could you call Mr. Campbell after practice?' So I'd call him," Schultz said. "He'd say, 'Let me read you the game report.' So he would read it to me and I would say, 'Well, that's not quite how it happened,' and I'd kind of give my version. So he'd say, 'OK, you'll be hearing from me.' I never heard from him. I never even got suspended."

Following the 1975–76 season, after the Canadiens swept the Flyers in four games in the Cup final, Schultz was traded to the Los Angeles Kings. He was devastated.

"Leaving the Flyers is something I look back on with a lot of disappointment," Schultz later said.

He would play four more seasons, with the Kings, the Pittsburgh Penguins and the Buffalo Sabres, and he never strayed from the combative style that made him successful, registering 405 penalty minutes and 27 fighting majors in 74 games in 1977–78.

Following his retirement in 1980, Schultz dabbled in coaching and running minor-league teams, and also started a successful limousine business in the Philadelphia area. He eventually became president of the Flyers alumni association, and often gives speeches about his days as the NHL's toughest enforcer.

Looking back on a career that spanned nine tough seasons, Schultz knows he left an indelible mark on the game he grew to love growing up on a farm in Saskatchewan.

"I played my role, but I also played pretty good hockey," Schultz said of his legacy as a player. "I was a small part of some great teams. It's just a fact that when you think of the Philadelphia Flyers and the 'Broad Street Bullies' of the '70s, you think about a number of guys, and I'm one of them. That's just the way it is. We were a good team, but we were tough, and I was one of the leaders in that department."

Dave Schultz

Position: Left wing
Date of birth: October 14, 1949
Place of birth: Waldheim, Saskatchewan

Season	Team	Lge	Regular Season					Playoffs				
			GP	G	A	Pts	PIM	GP	G	A	Pts	PIM
1969–70	Salem Rebels	EHL	67	32	37	69	356					
1969–70	Québec Aces	AHL	8	0	0	0	13	–	–	–	–	–
1970–71	Québec Aces	AHL	71	14	23	37	382	1	0	0	0	0
1971–72	Richmond Robins	AHL	76	18	28	46	392	–	–	–	–	–
1971–72	Philadelphia Flyers	NHL	1	0	0	0	0	–	–	–	–	–
1972–73	Philadelphia Flyers	NHL	76	9	12	21	259	11	1	0	1	51
1973–74	Philadelphia Flyers	NHL	73	20	16	36	348	17	2	4	6	139
1974–75	Philadelphia Flyers	NHL	76	9	17	26	472	17	2	3	5	83
1975–76	Philadelphia Flyers	NHL	71	13	19	32	307	16	2	2	4	90
1976–77	Los Angeles Kings	NHL	76	10	20	30	232	9	1	1	2	45
1977–78	Los Angeles Kings	NHL	8	2	0	2	27	·	–	–	–	–
1977–78	Pittsburgh Penguins	NHL	66	9	25	34	378	–	–	–	–	–
1978–79	Pittsburgh Penguins	NHL	47	4	9	13	157	–	–	–	–	–
1978–79	Buffalo Sabres	NHL	28	2	3	5	86	3	0	2	2	4
1979–80	Rochester Americans	AHL	56	10	14	24	24	4	1	0	1	12
1979–80	Buffalo Sabres	AHL	13	1	0	1	28	–	–	–	–	–
	NHL Totals		535	79	121	200	2294	73	8	12	20	412

Dave Schultz led the NHL in penalty minutes in 1972–73, 1973–74, 1974–75 and 1977–78. He also led the NHL in fights in 1972–73 (13 fights), 1974–75 (26), and 1977–78 (27).

Chapter Eleven

Chris Nilan

If a Hollywood scriptwriter sat down and tried to depict the life of an NHL enforcer, he'd be hard pressed to come up with a story as compelling as that of former Montréal Canadiens tough guy Chris "Knuckles" Nilan.

Any stereotype about NHL fighters that fans believe to be true actually is in Nilan's case: the rough neighborhood growing up, the street fights every weekend, that me-against-the world attitude, the fearlessness in fighting anyone and everyone to prove himself and, finally, that ticket to the big leagues that no one believed he would get.

Nilan overcame a disadvantage in the skills department through hard work and hard knocks, not only proving his worth as a fighter, but also playing on one of the best checking lines in modern NHL history with the Canadiens in the mid-1980s alongside greats Bob Gainey and Guy Carbonneau. Nilan even achieved the sort of storybook moment Hollywood loves when his name was engraved on the Stanley Cup in 1986.

But when Nilan was just a kid growing up in Boston's rough West Roxbury neighborhood, it was hard for anyone to imagine he would make a living on skates, although you didn't need to be a psychic to foresee he'd make a living with his fists.

"Chris was never a natural hockey player," said Nilan's father, Henry, a former Green Beret and paratrooper in the American military. "He always had to fight for what he got, in all meanings of the word. He always seemed to be willing to work harder, fight more and push more for what he wanted."

Nilan spent his childhood idolizing the great Boston Bruins teams of the 1970s, led by the incomparable defenseman Bobby Orr. Hockey was such a marginal sport in the Boston area before that era of greatness that there were few public rinks in the city for children and amateur leagues, so Nilan's first time on skates when he was five years old was on a frozen puddle in a parking lot near his house. But Orr's greatness made it so an entire generation of Boston kids grew up wanting to be hockey players, and rinks began popping up around the city like sprouts. One of those rinks was built just down the street from Nilan, and he immediately joined the neighborhood league.

In addition to Nilan's love of hockey, however, his youth was also defined by an uncanny knack for finding trouble.

"As a kid growing up in Boston, I fought a lot in the streets; I was constantly getting in fights. I just never backed down from anybody," Nilan recalled. "It was the type of neighborhood where if you let people push you around, you'd get pushed around."

Nilan displayed an uncommon fearlessness as a youngster. He recounted a time when he was sitting on the curb outside a local restaurant one summer night and two boys got out of a car. They immediately began taunting Nilan about his summer buzz cut before going into the restaurant to eat. An enraged Nilan pulled out the knife he used to carry with him at all times, slashed all four tires of the boys' car, and hid down the street to wait for them to come out. When they did, Nilan watched with joy as the boys vented their anger over the four flat tires. But a few nights later, at the same curb, those two boys got their revenge, giving Nilan a stern beating.

"That's just how I was," Nilan said, "I was always like that."

On the ice, Nilan was much the same. He was never the biggest or the most skilled player, so he had to prove his worth through sheer determination mixed with a little agitation.

"I was physical on the ice, but I didn't fight a lot when I first started playing hockey, just because I wasn't allowed," he said. "But as I got older, I was pretty mean on the ice. I had a take-no-prisoners attitude, and that really helped me."

When Nilan was a freshman at Catholic Memorial High School, he was nowhere near good enough to make the school's varsity hockey team. In fact, he barely got off the bench playing for the freshman team. Nilan made the junior varsity team as a sophomore, and played a regular shift on the squad his junior and senior years in high school. But despite the fact he had no reason to believe it, Nilan was always sure he would go far with hockey.

"All I ever had in my mind as a kid was that I wanted to be a hockey player and I wanted to play in the NHL," he said. "I used to sneak into Bruins games, I'd watch Bobby Orr just like everybody else. But my dream was to make the NHL, and I just had the confidence that I was going to do it."

Even though many of his coaches were unable to see that dogged ambition, Nilan credits one man for believing in his potential, his minor-league hockey coach, Paul King. When Nilan left to attend Northwood prep school in Lake Placid, New York, after his high school graduation, he exchanged letters with King the whole time. King had a lot of friends in the hockey world, and one of them was former Bruins tough guy Fernie Flaman, who was coaching the hockey team at Northeastern University in Boston. King convinced Flaman to come up to Lake Placid with him to see Nilan in action, and once Flaman saw the Nilan's bulldog attitude on the ice, he offered him a scholarship.

Nilan was far from being a standout athlete at Northeastern, playing a minor role his freshman year and getting 17 points in 20 games as a sophomore in 1977–78.

The summer following his sophomore season was Nilan's draft year, and he was convinced that some NHL team would take a chance on him. His father, Henry, and uncle, Eddie Carling, did not share Nilan's optimism.

"I tell the two of them that I'm going to get drafted," Nilan recalled their teasing, "then my father says to me, 'The only way you're going to get drafted is if there's another war.' Then my

uncle says, 'If you want a draft, go open that door
and you'll get a draft.' So they were both goofing
on me a whole lot."

But Nilan had the advantage of having his
mentor, King, in his corner. King, a judge, was
friendly with Montréal Canadiens legends
Dickie Moore and Doug Harvey because he had
helped the pair with their contracts during their
playing days.

"So Judge King asks Dickie Moore just to get
someone down there to see me play," Nilan said.
"Dickie Moore went to the Canadiens and asked
them to draft me, and they drafted me with one
of the last picks. But it was a favor."

Nilan was taken by legendary Canadiens general manager Sam Pollock as the 231st overall
pick in the 1978 draft, three picks shy of being
the last player chosen. Nilan played one more
season under Flaman at Northeastern before
heading up for his first Canadiens training camp
in the fall of 1979.

Nilan showed the Habs brass what he could do,
dropping his gloves every chance he got, but he
was sent to Montréal's top American Hockey
League farm club, the Nova Scotia Voyageurs.
Nilan sat out the first three games of that 1979–80
season, but on his first shift with the Voyageurs

he sent a message to the entire league that he would back down from no one.

The Nova Scotia Voyageurs were visiting the Maine Mariners in October of 1979, and the American team's biggest intimidator was defenceman Glen Cochrane. Voyageurs defenceman Tim Burke remembers that night well.

"That night in Maine, he went out and battled Glen Cochrane, the reigning heavyweight in the league at the time, to a standstill," Burke said. "That fight must have lasted two whole minutes, and by the end Cochrane had lost his sweater and was cut. All of his pads were off and he was just swinging bare-chested. Nilan showed us that night that we didn't have to worry about getting involved with physical teams like the Mariners, and we went on to do pretty well against Maine that year...it was amazing. Nilan just rolled through the league that year, fighting everybody until there were no challengers left."

After the Cochrane fight, Nilan became a favorite of Voyageurs coach Bert Templeton, and he became the Nova Scotia team's top enforcer from that point forward.

In February of 1980, the Canadiens decided they needed a little more toughness on their roster and called Nilan up from the minors. Though he didn't repeat his fiery debut with the Voyageurs when he played his first NHL game in Atlanta, Nilan would show what he was made of during his second game a few nights later in Philadelphia. In that game, Nilan chose Flyers winger Bob "Hound Dog" Kelly of Broad Street Bully fame as his first NHL dance partner.

"I put him down and that was it," Nilan said. "That was the start of the whole thing." Nilan played 15 games with the Canadiens that season, plus five more in the playoffs, and he would never be sent back to the AHL again.

Over the next three seasons, Nilan would fight practically every single time he was on the ice, but he couldn't earn himself a regular shift with the team. He often would be scratched for home games, and he felt Canadiens coach Bob Berry, who worked Nilan to the bone during practice, was unfairly singling him out.

Though today Nilan credits Berry with teaching him how to practice at the NHL level, he wasn't so grateful at the time, and he even stormed into Canadiens general manager Irving Grundman's office early in his career to demand a trade.

"I felt I could always play," Nilan said. "It was just a case of getting a chance to play with the right people."

That chance came when Jacques Lemaire was brought in to coach the Canadiens in February of the 1983–84 season. Lemaire saw something in Nilan that Berry and Claude Ruel before him didn't. He almost immediately placed Nilan on the right wing with his top two defensive forwards, captain Bob Gainey and center Guy Carbonneau, and over the next three years, they were the top checking line in the NHL. In 1984–85, his first full season with his new linemates, Nilan finished with a career-high 21 goals and 16 assists, but he never forgot his enforcer role, piling up a Canadiens-record 358 penalty minutes as well.

"I felt good about that, but I knew I had to keep doing my job the other way. It was fruitless not to do what got me here," Nilan said of his newfound success. "Jacques Lemaire basically told me, 'Don't start thinking you're a goal-scorer now.' "

Lemaire instilled a sense of confidence in Nilan by using him in all game situations, including power plays, and by working individually with him on his skills after practices. But Lemaire never liked living in the fishbowl of the Montréal media, and after the 1984–85 season, he stepped down as head coach to join the Canadiens front office. Lemaire's replacement was a rookie, Jean Perron, and he was inheriting a team in transition.

The 1985–86 Canadiens had a corc of veterans, including Nilan, Gainey, Carbonneau, Larry Robinson, Mario Tremblay, Bobby Smith and Mats Naslund. But there also was an unusual amount of first-and second-year players on that team for a franchise that prided itself on integrating young players into the lineup slowly.

Nilan's year got off to a rough start when, during an early-season game against his boyhood team, the Boston Bruins, he received a rare 10-minute penalty (resulting in a 10-minute power play) for butt-ending Bruins star Rick Middleton in the face. Nilan insists to this day he didn't butt-end Middleton, that he gave him a backhander with his glove, and since he was holding his stick when he did, it looked like a butt-end. Regardless, the NHL saw fit to suspend Nilan for 10 games.

That incident only intensified what already was a bitter rivalry between the Canadiens and the Bruins, and Nilan became public enemy number one in his hometown.

"But those guys were scared [stiff] after that," Nilan said. "They didn't know what I would do next, and to who."

As a reaction to the Middleton incident, the Bruins called up career minor-league tough guy Jay Miller to counter Nilan, and over the next three seasons the two would lock horns almost every time they played. Nilan still remembers the first match-up of what would be dozens of on-ice encounters.

"I got put on the ice, they put him on the ice in Boston," Nilan said. "I went up to him and said, 'I know what you're here for,' and I dropped my gloves and just fought him right away. I figured, let's get it over with. We fought a lot, and they were good fights."

The Canadiens got off to a slow start in 1985–86 as it took some time for the club's veterans and young players to jell.

During a West Coast road trip in February of 1986, Nilan got into a fight with talented rookie winger Stéphane Richer in practice one day. Nilan had resented Richer more or less all season because he felt his teammate was wasting his considerable talent by displaying a lack of effort in practices and games. On this day, Richer made the mistake of retaliating for a body check Nilan laid on him in the corner, and he paid the price by taking a few Nilan punches before their teammates stepped in to break up the scrap. Curiously, that incident seemed to ignite the Canadiens and bring them closer together. The newly formed team spirit, coupled with the emergence of rookie goalie Patrick Roy, brought the Canadiens their 23rd Stanley Cup in team history.

Though Nilan would set an NHL playoff record that year with 141 penalty minutes, he was forced to miss the last two games of the Cup final against the Calgary Flames after he tore ligaments in his ankle while fighting Neil Sheehy in game three. The injury denied him a chance to skate around the hallowed Montréal Forum ice with the Stanley Cup.

"I would have loved to be out on the ice with those guys," Nilan said. "But it was really special to me to know that I was a part of that."

Unfortunately for Nilan, the next two seasons under Perron were difficult to the point where, midway through the 1987–88 season, he and the coach had a confrontation in front of the whole team. It didn't take long for general manager Serge Savard to side with the coach and ship Nilan to the New York Rangers in exchange for the option of swapping first-round picks at the next entry draft.

Nilan said Bruins defenseman Ray Bourque saw him after that season ended and told him how much of an impact his trade had.

"Once you left, we knew we could beat those guys," Nilan remembers Bourque telling him of the Canadiens. "We were walking on eggshells whenever you played."

Nilan spent the next two years in New York and even signed with his hometown Bruins in 1990. It was with Boston that Nilan would set a new record for penalties in a game with 10 against the Hartford Whalers on March 31, 1991, including six minors, two majors, one misconduct and one game misconduct. But Nilan was never the same player, never regained the confidence he displayed in Montréal.

"I was never the same after I left Montréal," he said. "I was real messed up after that."

During the 1991–92 season, with Nilan playing uninspired hockey, the Bruins placed him on waivers and he was picked up by Savard and the Canadiens.

Nilan was rejuvenated by his return to Montréal and helped the Canadiens through the stretch drive and into the playoffs, where they were swept in the second round by Boston.

He retired after that season wearing the same jersey he was given 13 years earlier when he attended his first NHL training camp as a young ruffian expected to do little more than fight. As Chris Nilan walked off into the sunset at the end of his storied career, he had proven he could do a whole lot more than that.

Chris Nilan

Position: Right wing
Date of birth: February 9, 1958
Place of birth: Boston, Massachusetts

Season	Team	Lge	Regular Season					Playoffs				
			GP	G	A	Pts	PIM	GP	G	A	Pts	PIM
1976–77	Northeastern University	NCAA	20	3	2	5	0					
1977–78	Northeastern University	NCAA	20	8	9	17	0					
1978–79	Northeastern University	NCAA	26	9	17	26	92					
1979–80	Nova Scotia Voyageurs	AHL	49	15	10	25	304	–	–	–	–	–
1979–80	Montréal Canadiens	NHL	15	0	2	2	50	5	0	0	0	2
1980–81	Montréal Canadiens	NHL	57	7	8	15	262	2	0	0	0	0
1981–82	Montréal Canadiens	AHL	49	7	4	11	204	5	1	1	2	22
1982–83	Montréal Canadiens	NHL	66	6	8	14	213	3	0	0	0	5
1983–84	Montréal Canadiens	NHL	76	16	10	26	338	15	1	0	1	81
1984–85	Montréal Canadiens	NHL	77	21	16	37	358	12	2	1	3	81
1985–86	Montréal Canadiens	NHL	72	19	15	34	274	18	1	2	3	141
1986–87	Montréal Canadiens	NHL	44	4	16	20	266	17	3	0	3	75
1987–88	Montréal Canadiens	NHL	50	7	5	12	209	–	–	–	–	–
1987–88	New York Rangers	NHL	22	3	5	8	961	–	–	–	–	–
1988–89	New York Rangers	NHL	38	7	7	14	77	4	4	1	1	28
1989–90	New York Rangers	NHL	25	1	2		59	4	4	1	1	19
1990–91	Boston Bruins	NHL	41	6	9	15	277	19	19	2	2	62
1991–92	Boston Bruins	NHL	39	5	5	10	186	–	–	–	–	–
1991–92	Montréal Canadiens	NHL	17	1	3	4	74	7	7	1	1	15
	NHL Totals		688	110	115	225	3043	111	8	9	17	531

Chris Nilan was the fastest player in history to reach 3000 career penalty minutes, and his average of 4.42 per game is the highest among players with at least 2500 career penalty minutes.

Chapter Twelve

Eddie Shack

There may have been tougher players who have suited up for the Toronto Maple Leafs, but no player had the ability to rile his opposition, to burrow under their skin and to induce rage quite like Eddie Shack.

Shack was the cause of one of the bloodiest, most brutal fights in NHL history while he played for the New York Rangers early in his career. Detroit Red Wings superstar Gordie Howe and a few of his teammates had taken to roughing up the young Shack for much of the 1959 game. Rangers tough guy Lou Fontinato challenged Howe to a fight in an attempt to stick up for his teammate. Howe re-arranged Fontinato's face in a fight that is talked about to this day among hockey connoisseurs.

But Shack was also one of the biggest crowd-pleasers in NHL history. His flair earned him the nickname the "Entertainer." Whenever he was

chosen as one of the three stars at Maple Leaf
Gardens, Shack would sprint to center ice and
do a pirouette for the crowd. Although Toronto
coach George "Punch" Imlach didn't particularly
like putting Shack out on the ice, his hand was
sometimes forced by the Maple Leaf faithful
chanting, "We want Shack!"

Shack is also one of the few players to have
a song written for him. One night during a game
against the Rangers, Shack hit Rod Gilbert with an
elbow and cross-checked Phil Goyette in the head
on the same play without drawing a penalty,
despite the fact the blows left both men lying
unconscious on the ice. Toronto reporter Paul
Rimstead referred to the incident in his game story,
and the newspaper the next day had the headline:
"Clear the track, here comes Shack." Hockey
writer and historian Brian McFarlane was so
inspired by the headline that he wrote a song with
the phrase as the chorus. The tune became popular, going to number one on the charts in 1966.

Shack's journey to the NHL began practically on
a whim. As a teenager in Sudbury, Ontario, he
worked in a coal mine and for a local butcher when
he decided to give hockey a shot. He tried out for
the Guelph Biltmores in 1952. Within five years he
was the team's best player, leading them to a berth
in the Memorial Cup tournament in 1957.

Shack intrigued the New York Rangers, and they sent him to their American Hockey League farm club, the Providence Reds, for the 1957–58 season. While in Providence, Shack summoned the rage of the AHL's reigning heavyweight at the time, Larry Zeidel, and the two engaged in a vicious stick fight one night. Both players were thrown out of the game, went to shower and change, then returned to the stands to watch the game's conclusion. Zeidel saw Shack sitting in the front row, and the two continued their on-ice battle in the stands, with both men throwing punches surrounded by the fans.

The Rangers called Shack up to the NHL in 1958–59, expecting him to light up the league. Alas, over the next two seasons Shack proved a disappointment, and he was eventually dealt to the Leafs in 1960 for Pat Hannigan and Johnny Wilson. Toronto proved a perfect fit for Shack, as he and the Leafs won the first of three straight Stanley Cups during his first full season with the team in 1961–62.

Shack, who was big for his era at 6'1" and 195 pounds, made a habit of picking on the other team's smallest players. In a game against the Chicago Blackhawks, defenceman Pat Stapleton—all 5'8", 180 pounds of him—tried to give Shack a hip check. Shack retaliated by kneeing Stapleton in the back and whacking him across the head with his stick, leaving Stapleton to crawl back to his bench.

One of Shack's favorite stories involves his habit of going after Montréal Canadiens center Henri Richard, nicknamed the "Pocket Rocket" because he was Maurice "the Rocket" Richard's younger brother and he was only 5'7", 160 pounds. Shack didn't appreciate how liberally the diminutive Richard was zipping all over the ice, and one night decided to drop the gloves with him. Shack got a couple of punches in when Richard grabbed his arms to tie him up. That didn't stop Shack, though, and he head-butted Richard just above the eye, cutting him for six stitches.

"Let's see if the little bugger can take it," Shack remembers telling himself. "So I bonked him with my head."

Later on in the same game, Shack showed that he didn't only go after smaller players when he checked the monstrous Jean Béliveau into the boards, knocking him out of action for the next two games.

Eddie Shack would go on to play for the Boston Bruins, Los Angeles Kings, Buffalo Sabres and Pittsburgh Penguins. He returned to the Leafs for his final two seasons before retiring in 1975 with 1439 penalty minutes in 1047 games.

Eddie Shack

Position: Forward
Date of birth: February 11, 1937
Place of birth: Sudbury, Ontario

Season	Team	Lge	Regular Season					Playoffs				
			GP	G	A	Pts	PIM	GP	G	A	Pts	PIM
1952–53	Guelph Biltmores	OHA	21	2	6	8	0					
1953–54	Guelph Biltmores	OHA	Statistics Unavailable									
1954–55	Guelph Biltmores	OHA	19	6	7	13	0					
1955–56	Guelph Biltmores	OHA	52	47	57	104	0					
1956–57	Providence Reds	AHL	35	16	18	34	98	–	–	–	–	–
1957–58	New York Rangers	NHL	67	7	14	21	109	–	–	–	–	–
1958–59	Springfield Indians	AHL	9	3	4	7	10	–	–	–	–	–
1959–60	New York Rangers	NHL	62	8	10	18	110	–	–	–	–	–
1959–60	New York Rangers	NHL	12	1	2	3	17	–	–	–	–	–
1960–61	Toronto Maple Leafs	NHL	55	14	14	28	0	4	0	0	0	2
1960–61	Toronto Maple Leafs	NHL	44	7	14	21	62	9	0	0	0	18
1962–63	Toronto Maple Leafs	NHL	63	16	9	25	97	10	2	1	3	11
1963–64	Toronto Maple Leafs	NHL	64	11	10	21	128	13	0	1	1	25
1964–65	Toronto Maple Leafs	NHL	67	5	9	14	68	5	1	0	1	8
1965–66	Rochester Americans	NHL	8	3	4	7	12	–	–	–	–	–
1965–66	Toronto Maple Leafs	AHL	63	26	17	43	88	4	2	1	3	33
1966–67	Toronto Maple Leafs	NHL	63	11	14	25	58	8	0	0	0	8
1967–68	Boston Bruins	NHL	70	23	19	42	107	4	0	1	1	6
1968–69	Boston Bruins	NHL	50	11	11	22	74	9	0	2	2	23
1970–71	Los Angeles Kings	NHL	73	22	12	34	115	–	–	–	–	–
1970–71	Los Angeles Kings	NHL	11	2	2	4		–	–	–	–	–
1971–72	Buffalo Sabres	NHL	56	25	17	42	93	–	–	–	–	–
1971–72	Buffalo Sabres	NHL	50	11	14	25	34	–	–	–	–	–
1972–73	Pittsburgh Penguins	NHL	18	5	9	14	12	4	0	1	1	15
1973–74	Pittsburgh Penguins	NHL	74	25	20	45	84	–	–	–	–	–
1974–75	Toronto Maple Leafs	NHL	5	7	8	15	74	4	1	0	1	2
1974–75	Oklahoma City Blazers	CHL	8	3	4	7	10	–	–	–	–	–
1975–76	Toronto Maple Leafs	NHL	26	2	1	3	11	–	–	–	–	–
1976–77	Whitby Warriors	OHA	9	5	4	9	8					
	NHL Totals		1047	239	226	465	1439	74	6	7	13	151

Although Eddie Shack's own penalty-minute totals are by no means staggering, his grating style of play threw many of his opponents into fits of rage, making him probably the greatest agitator of his generation.

Chapter Thirteen

Sprague Cleghorn

All those people who say that fighting has always been a part of the game are primarily referring to Sprague Cleghorn. Cleghorn was a terror on the blue line in the early years of the NHL, one who fought his battles both with his fists and his stick.

Cleghorn spent his Hall of Fame career playing for the Ottawa Senators, Toronto St. Pats, Montréal Canadiens and Boston Bruins from 1918 to 1928. Before that, he played for a number of other professional teams, starting in 1909, when he moved from his native Montréal to play two seasons in New York City.

When Cleghorn began his NHL career, there were only three teams in the league, and they were all in Canada. By the time he retired, the league had expanded to 10 teams, with six of them in the United States, and a major reason for that rapid expansion was the stellar and often brutal play of Cleghorn.

"He was a product of a rough neighborhood where everything you got, you had to fight for," former NHL referee Bobby Hewiston once said of Cleghorn. "He played hockey the same way. You could be sure Sprague was well fitted for it."

He was the top defenseman on nearly every team he played for, and Cleghorn's abrasive style led to Stanley Cup victories in Ottawa in 1920 and 1921, and in Montréal in 1924.

Despite his tremendous skill, Cleghorn's legacy has been defined by tales of his nasty temper on the ice and the incredibly protective way he watched over his younger brother Odie, a high-scoring winger who was Sprague's teammate with both the Montréal Canadiens and the pre-NHL Montréal Wanderers.

One of the earliest and most vicious examples of this brotherly duty came on December 12, 1912, when the Wanderers traveled to Toronto to play an exhibition game against the cross-town rival Canadiens and their star player, Newsy Lalonde. About halfway through the game, Lalonde slammed Odie into the boards hard, prompting Sprague to skate clear across the ice and plough into Lalonde's forehead with his stick. The quick strike barely missed Lalonde's eye, and he needed 12 stitches to close the wound. Toronto authorities didn't take kindly to Cleghorn's use of his stick and summoned him to court, slapping him with a $50 fine in addition to the $50 fine he received from National Hockey Association president Emmett Quinn. Quinn also suspended Cleghorn for four weeks, but he was back in the Wanderers lineup after sitting out only one game.

Following Cleghorn's second Stanley Cup victory with the Senators in 1921, he was reunited with his younger brother when he was traded to the Canadiens, a team that already boasted several stars in Lalonde, Georges Vézina, Didier Pitre and Billy Coutu, to name a few. The pairing of Coutu and Cleghorn on the Canadiens blue line was not only the most dominant defence in the league, but it was also the scariest.

Canadiens general manager Leo Dandurand appointed Cleghorn as his team leader (what would be called the captain today), and it didn't take long for the ornery Cleghorn to show his new teammates how he was wired. The Canadiens were playing the Senators on February 1, 1922, and Cleghorn was still carrying a grudge against the team that traded him after he helped lead them to the Stanley Cup. Cleghorn first unleashed his rage that night on Senators star defenceman Eddie Gerard, opening up a five-stitch cut just above his eye and knocking him out of the game. Next came Ottawa sniper Frank Nighbor, who was also sent off after a Cleghorn check sent him sprawling, injuring his elbow. Finally, Cleghorn put the butt of his stick in the face of Senators forward Cy Denneny, bloodying his nose and the area just above his eye.

The Senators appealed to NHL president Frank Calder to have Cleghorn barred for life from the league, but the Toronto St. Pats and the Hamilton Tigers didn't agree, and a unanimous vote was needed for such a punishment.

Francis "King" Clancy was a Senators rookie that year, and watching Cleghorn on his rampage had a profound effect on the future Hall of Fame forward.

"He was just a terrible man to have to play against, a terrific stick-handler, a master with the butt-end, and tough," Clancy once said. "Holy Jesus, he was tough."

Clancy remembers one game where Cleghorn was racing toward his net on a rush when Clancy banged his stick on the ice, pretending to be a teammate requesting a pass. Cleghorn sent the puck to Clancy, who immediately began rushing in the opposite direction.

"So when the period was over, I was feeling pretty good as I walked to our dressing room," Clancy recalled. "The fans were applauding me, and just as I was going in the room, I heard this friendly voice: 'King,' and I turned around to see who it was. Well, I want to tell you, my friend, did I ever get a sweet wallop in the kisser. It was Sprague all right, just quietly turning off my lights. Jesus, did he hit me a beauty."

In the 1923 playoffs, Cleghorn attacked an Ottawa defenseman so viciously that his own team suspended him. Manager Dandurand described the incident as something "befitting an animal."

The following year, the Canadiens welcomed Howie Morenz to the team and captured the franchise's second of 24 Stanley Cups. But a gaffe by Cleghorn almost led to the cherished Cup being lost on Montréal's streets. The Canadiens were getting ready to celebrate their Cup victory with a party at Dandurand's home in Montréal's posh Westmount neighborhood, and Cleghorn, with teammates Sylvio Mantha and Georges Vézina, got a ride with their boss in his Model T.

But the streets of Montréal were particularly snowy that day, and Dandurand's car had trouble making the uphill voyage while loaded with professional athletes. Cleghorn rode with the

Cup on his lap, but he had placed it on the curb when he and his teammates got out of the car to give it a push—and forgot to pick it up when he got back in.

Hours later, while the team was celebrating, Dandurand's wife asked to see the famous Cup they had fought so hard to win. That's when Cleghorn realized what happened, and he immediately got back into the car with Dandurand to fetch the Cup. Miraculously, the trophy was sitting exactly where Cleghorn had left it.

Cleghorn retired as a member of the Boston Bruins in 1928, but not before serving as a big influence on a young Eddie Shore, who would go on to take over his mantle as the league's best combination of rough play and talent.

Sprague Cleghorn

Position: Defence
Date of birth: March 11, 1890
Place of birth: Montréal, Québec

Season	Team	Lge	Regular Season					Playoffs				
			GP	G	A	Pts	PIM	GP	G	A	Pts	PIM
1918–19	Ottawa Senators	NHL	18	6	6	12	27					
1919–20	Ottawa Senators	NHL	21	16	5	21	62					
1920–21	Ottawa Senators	NHL	3	2	1	3	9					
1920–21	Toronto St. Pats	NHL	13	3	4	7	26					
1921–22	Montréal Canadiens	NHL	24	17	7	24	63					
1922–23	Montréal Canadiens	NHL	24	9	4	13	34					
1923–24	Montréal Canadiens	NHL	23	8	3	11	39					
1924–25	Montréal Canadiens	NHL	27	8	1	9	82					
1925–26	Boston Bruins NHL	NHL	28	6	5	11	49					
1926–27	Boston Bruins NHL	NHL	44	7	1	8	84					
1927–28	Boston Bruins NHL	NHL	26	2	2	4	14					
1928–29	Newark Bulldogs	CAHL	3	0	0	0	0					
	NHL Totals		251	84	39	123	489					

In his first season with the Montréal Canadiens, defenceman Sprague Cleghorn showcased his incredible skill in all areas of the game. He finished first in the league in penalty minutes and eighth in both goals and points, as a defenceman no less.

Chapter Fourteen

Tie Domi

As a youngster growing up in Belle River, Ontario, Tie Domi found a perfect role model in Dave "Tiger" Williams.

In the late 1970s, Williams was the NHL's pre-eminent enforcer for the Toronto Maple Leafs, a terror on the ice who made his opponents accountable for their actions, a player who would become the NHL's all-time leader in penalty minutes.

Domi admired Williams for his combative nature and his showman's instincts, but the main thing Domi saw in "Tiger" was himself. Domi, like Williams, has never been a big man, but he never let that stop him from becoming his generation's top enforcer, one who made a career out of dropping the gloves against bigger men and coming out on top.

It is unlikely, however, that even Domi could foresee this successful future while growing up in Belle River, a small community near Windsor, Ontario. Domi, the youngest of three children, grew up playing football and soccer against his older brothers and their friends, who were often five years older than he was. But that mattered little to the young Domi, because he was born with toughness in his blood.

Tahir (Tie) Domi's father, John, and mother, Meryem, were Albanian immigrants. John Domi came to Canada in the 1950s after fleeing communist Albania. As the elder Domi escaped his native country into Greece, he was shot just above the right eye. John Domi never had that bullet removed from his head, keeping it as a reminder of why he moved to Canada and what it took for him to get there.

"He was fearless," Domi says. "He escaped from Albania with nothing when he came here, and he worked to get everything he had to give his family a good life."

Though Domi inherited his toughness from his father, one thing he didn't have in those genes was height. Domi has been listed at 5'10" throughout his NHL career, but even he would admit that's being generous. Considering Domi's favorite adversary over the course of his career was the 6'3", 225-pound Bob Probert, playing the role of enforcer at that height is no easy task.

And that's exactly what the NHL scouts who saw him play junior hockey in Peterborough, Ontario, thought as well, but Domi just didn't listen to them.

"I had to fight my way into the league," Domi says. "They said I was too small to be a tough guy. So I had to beat those odds to just get a shot at the NHL. But I don't mind that. I've always had to prove myself, every year. That hasn't changed my whole life."

Despite his perceived lack of size, Domi was intriguing enough as a prospect that the Toronto Maple Leafs used their second-round pick in the 1988 NHL draft to select him 27th overall, long before perennial all-stars like Tony Amonte, Mark Recchi and Rob Blake, who were all taken in the fourth round that year.

After a final year in junior, Domi made his NHL debut with the Leafs in 1989–90, getting into a fight and picking up 37 minutes in penalties in his first game and enraging Detroit Red Wings coach Jacques Demers with his taunting to the point that Demers himself became scrappy and tried to climb the glass in a vain attempt to get at Leafs coach Doug Carpenter. The Leafs, however, gave up on Domi after that

season, trading him to the New York Rangers in
June 1990.

During a February 5, 1991, contest with the
Rangers against the hated New York Islanders,
Domi had one of the best games of his career to
that point, scoring the game-winning goal while
getting an assist and winning two fights. Domi
was on cloud nine as he came off the ice that
night when Rangers head coach Roger Neilson
called him into his office and delivered some
horrible news.

"I thought I was getting sent to the minors,"
Domi recalls. "[Neilson] said to me, 'Your father
passed away at nine o'clock tonight.' He'd seen
part of the game, he was playing cards with his
friends. I think he was probably pretty proud of
me that night."

John Domi died of a heart attack at age 62, on
a night one the younger Domi calls the worst of
his life, despite his heroics on the ice. Domi was
devastated and still feels a certain degree of
regret about how his father left him.

"I still feel to this day I never really told him
how much I loved him," Domi said seven years
after his father's death. "I hadn't seen him, I had
only been home for Christmas for about a day
[that year]. I called him and my mom every day."

Domi eventually decided to put those emotions into his game, and it made him an instant fan favorite in New York. It was on Broadway, appropriately enough, that Domi's penchant for showmanship took hold, once emulating his hero Williams by riding his stick like a broom after scoring a goal. Rangers crowds at Madison Square Garden fell in love with the diminutive tough guy who not only won more fights than he lost but also won them with style.

"When we're in our building, the fans cheer me," Domi said. "Then, when I go on the road, the fans are always booing me. To me, that says I'm doing my job. That's the bottom line."

Domi's favorite move after winning a bout was to hit an imaginary speed punching bag on his way to the penalty box. But his most famous post-fight celebration, by far, came on February 9, 1992. Ever since Domi had entered the league three years earlier, he had wanted to test his skills against the NHL's reigning heavyweight at the time, the Detroit Red Wings' menacing forward Bob Probert. That February night, 10 minutes into the hockey game, Domi finally got his chance with Probert and cut him over the eye in an epic punch-up that lasted nearly 90 seconds. In Domi's estimation, he won the fight hands down.

As he made his way to the penalty box, after prying himself loose from the linesman, Domi repeatedly gestured toward his waist as if he was wearing the heavyweight championship belt. Though the Ranger fans in attendance that night loved it, the Red Wings were not thrilled with Domi's showboating, and an all-out brawl broke out between the two teams as soon as Domi took his seat in the box.

That fight put Domi on the map, and the anticipation was heavy for the next Rangers game against the Red Wings about one month later. Domi, however, was hobbled with a knee injury by the time that rematch came up and couldn't make it into the lineup.

"I heard that a lot of people were looking forward to this game," Domi said at the time. "All I can say is that Bob Probert will be in the league next year. I'll be in the league next year. There will be other games, other meetings."

That next meeting was to come the following season, on December 2, 1992. About a week before the game, a reporter asked Domi whether he was aware of when Detroit was coming up on the schedule. Domi responded honestly and said yes, which is more than understandable considering the task he would have to take on that night.

The conversation with the reporter continued and Domi said some things that were perceived throughout the hockey world as pre-fight hype, a serious no-no in the NHL. Fighting is tolerated in the league, but only because it is seen as a spontaneous release of tension that could potentially avoid a seriously violent incident. Premeditated fighting, however, is deemed unacceptable.

Regardless, Domi's message was heard loud and clear by fans and the media. The day of the game, USA Today and a New York tabloid ran a "Tale of the Tape," with Domi and Probert on the front page of their respective sports sections, and both men understood that a fight was inevitable.

Domi and Probert dropped the gloves 37 seconds into the game, and Probert, by some estimates, threw at least 40 punches in one of the most entertaining and most-discussed fights in recent history. Although the NHL frowned on how the fight came about, with Domi being fined $500 and suspended for two days for hyping the clash, Domi's coach Neilson did not share that opinion.

"I thought it was a great fight," Neilson said after the game, a 5–3 Rangers victory. "When people are going home tonight, that's one of the things for sure they'll be talking about. It sure pumped everybody up."

It was around this time, in the early '90s, that the NHL began a campaign to slowly take fighting out of the game, or at least to make it a less important part. The season after that infamous fight, Domi was once again traded, this time to the Winnipeg Jets. Rangers general manager Neil Smith explained his decision to trade Domi and fellow tough guy Kris King for skilled center Ed Olczyk by saying that the game had less and less room for fighters.

"Tie is Tie—one of a kind," Smith said at the time. "But our game is changing, and we've got to change with it. There are a lot more skilled players in the game and a faster tempo. In all due respect to Tie, he couldn't get into our lineup. It's all well and good to be popular, but you've got to get into games."

Domi was welcomed with open arms when he arrived in Winnipeg after Jets star rookie Teemu Selanne had a stick broken over his back during a game with the Minnesota North Stars the night before the trade. Upon seeing Domi enter the Jets dressing room for the first time, Selanne gave him a big hug.

The arrival of Domi and King is directly linked to Selanne's wild success that 1992–93 season, when he established a new NHL rookie record with 76 goals. At the time of the Domi trade on December 28, however, Selanne only had 28 goals, meaning he scored a whopping 46 goals between New Year's Day and the end of the season, helped largely by the respect he was getting from the opposition as a result of the mere presence of Domi and King.

Olczyk, for the record, managed to score only 18 goals with 32 assists in 103 games over two and a half seasons for Smith and the Rangers before being sent back to the Jets in 1994–95. Over the same span in Winnipeg, Domi had 15 goals, 24 assists and 724 penalty minutes in 161 games for the Jets.

Domi only lasted one full season in Winnipeg, piling up 347 penalty minutes in 81 games in 1993–94, before being traded back to the team drafted him, the Toronto Maple Leafs, near the end of the 1994–95 season.

It was with Toronto that Domi began looking seriously at his role, and quickly realized his career would have a short shelf life if he didn't improve other aspects of his game. He began taking advantage of his strong skating stride to become an elite forechecker, and soon became a player who didn't necessarily have to drop the gloves to be effective. Which doesn't mean Domi all of

a sudden stopped sticking up for his teammates.
A former Leaf once recounted a story that described
Domi's extremely protective nature quite well.

Domi and a bunch of his teammates were in
a bar in Chicago one night when a group of U.S.
Marines came in and began harassing a couple of
Leafs players. Domi confronted the Marines and
asked what the problem was, and they responded
that it was none of his business.

"It is now," Domi told the Marine.

The Marines and Domi agreed that the biggest
of their group would get a free punch to Domi's
head, and then Domi could reply.

"This guy hauls back and punches Tie in the
face," the teammate remembers, "and Tie looks
at him and says, 'That's not your best shot, I'll
give you one more.' Now, I can tell this guy has
broken his hand and his buddies are like, 'It
looks like we picked on the wrong midget.' He
can't punch with his right, so he gives Tie a little
baby punch with his left hand, and then Tie
must have hit this guy 50 times. He was begging
Tie to stop."

Despite that colorful story, in Toronto, Domi
actually became a player who could contribute
in other areas of the game, which made him

a valuable player for the Leafs, even in the play-offs, when fights are less common.

"I think, and this is my own subjective opinion, that he was part showman early on, and part of his show was his ability to scrap," Pat Quinn, who coached the Leafs from 1998 to 2006, once said of Domi. "I don't mind scrapping, but I like the guys to be able to play, as well, and that was my message to Tie, that he had some skills that would allow him to be a decent player if he'd just push himself in practice and not just rely on two-and-a-half minutes of showtime to keep a job in the National Hockey League."

Domi became the league's elite enforcer in Toronto because of how effective a player he became with his gloves on, while remaining a vicious opponent with his gloves off.

"I respect him for the way he plays," said fellow enforcer Chris Simon, a giant of a man at 6'3", 220 pounds. "He's doing a big man's job, and he's a small guy. He could be the toughest guy for his size in the league, pound for pound. He's fighting guys my size all the time."

But for all the accolades and respect Domi earned for his willingness to take on anyone and everyone, his tenure in Toronto was marked by moments where he failed to use his head.

"Fifty per cent of the time I fight just for the sake of fighting, to get things going, it's situational," Domi said. "But when I get really mad, I don't have too much control. That's just always been in me."

Domi demonstrated that lack of control on several occasions for the Leafs, starting early in his first season with the team when he sucker-punched Rangers defenseman Ulf Samuelsson, earning himself an eight-game suspension.

The lack of control was once again evident in the second round of the 2001 playoffs, when the Leafs faced the New Jersey Devils. With only 7.3 seconds left in game four of the series and Toronto ahead 3–1, Domi came out of nowhere and elbowed the Devils' star defenseman, Scott Niedermayer, in the head while the puck was at the other end of the ice.

The elbow knocked Niedermayer out for the rest of the series and made Domi public enemy number one in the NHL as columnists across the continent ripped him for delivering a cheap shot to one of the game's greatest stars. Domi was suspended for the rest of the series and—because Toronto lost in seven games—for the first eight games of the 2001–02 season, as well. But Domi showed he would not allow his punishment to change the way he played, and he got into a fight during his second game back from the suspension.

Despite the momentary lapses in reason, Domi has persevered in his role like almost no other enforcer ever has. In 1997–98, Domi broke his childhood idol Tiger Williams' Toronto franchise record for penalty minutes in a season when he compiled 365 in 80 games, and on December 15, 2001, he passed Williams to become the Maple Leafs' all-time penalty-minute leader when he pounded Montréal's Reid Simpson in a fight.

But Domi's most incredible achievement came on March 3, 2006, when he played his 1000th career NHL game, a mark only one other true enforcer—Craig Berube—ever reached, outlasting the likes of Probert, Williams, Terry O'Reilly, Chris Nilan, Dave Schultz and all the other designated fighters. Over the course of those 1000 games, Domi dropped his gloves 268 times.

Domi's wife, Leanne, and his three children, who never had the opportunity to meet Domi's father, the inspiration behind his toughness, were all at Toronto's Air Canada Center that night to celebrate the remarkable milestone.

"Pretty good," Domi said shortly before playing that game, "for a guy who wasn't supposed to make it, eh?"

Pretty good, indeed.

Tie Domi

Position: Right wing
Date of birth: November 1, 1969
Place of birth: Windsor, Ontario

Season	Team	Lge	Regular Season					Playoffs				
			GP	G	A	Pts	PIM	GP	G	A	Pts	PIM
1986–87	Peterborough Petes	OHL	18	1	1	2	79	10	0	0	0	20
1987–88	Peterborough Petes	OHL	60	22	21	43	292	12	3	9	12	24
1987–88	Peterborough Petes	OHL	43	14	16	30	175	17	10	9	19	70
1988–89	Newmarket Saints	AHL	57	14	11	25	285	–	–	–	–	–
1989–90	Toronto Maple Leafs	NHL	2	0	0	0	42	–	–	–	–	–
1989–90	Binghampton Rangers	AHL	25	11	6	17	219	7	3	2	5	16
1990–91	New York Rangers	NHL	28	1	0	1	185	–	–	–	–	–
1990–91	New York Rangers	NHL	42	2	4	6	246	6	1	1	2	32
1991–92	New York Rangers	NHL	12	2	0	2	95	–	–	–	–	–
1992–93	Winnipeg Jets	NHL	49	3	10	13	249	6	1	0	1	23
1993–94	Winnipeg Jets	NHL	81	8	11	19	347	–	–	–	–	–
1994–95	Winnipeg Jets	NHL	31	4	4	8	128	–	–	–	–	–
1994–95	Toronto Maple Leafs	NHL	9	0	1	1	31	7	1	0	1	0
1995–96	Toronto Maple Leafs	NHL	72	7	6	13	297	6	0	2	2	4
1996–97	Toronto Maple Leafs	NHL	80	1	17	28	275	–	–	–	–	–
1997–98	Toronto Maple Leafs	NHL	80	4	10	14	365	–	–	–	–	–
1998–99	Toronto Maple Leafs	NHL	72	8	14	22	198	14	0	2	2	24
2000–01	Toronto Maple Leafs	NHL	70	5	9	14	198	12	0	1	1	20
2001–02	Toronto Maple Leafs	NHL	82	13	7	20	214	8	0	1	1	20
2002–03	Toronto Maple Leafs	NHL	74	9	10	19	157	19	1	3	4	61
2003–04	Toronto Maple Leafs	NHL	79	15	14	29	171	7	1	0	1	13
2004–05	Toronto Maple Leafs	NHL	80	7	13	20	208	13	2	2	4	41
2005–06	Toronto Maple Leafs	NHL	77	5	11	16	109	–	–	–	–	–
	NHL Totals		1020	104	141	245	3515	98	7	12	19	238

Tie Domi sits third on the NHL's all-time penalty minutes list, 451 shy of his idol and all-time leader Dave "Tiger" Williams, who sits at 3966.

Notes on Sources

Allen, Kevin. *Crunch*. Chicago: Triumph Books, 1999.

Diamond, Dan (ed). *Total NHL*. Toronto: Dan Diamond and Associates Inc., 2003.

Goyens, Chrys and Turoweitz, Allan. *Lions in Winter*. Whitby, Ontario: McGraw-Hill Ryerson Ltd., 1994.

Fischler, Stan. *Hockey's 100*. New York: Beaufort Books Inc., 1984.

Fischler, Stan. *The Ultimate Bad Boys*. Toronto: Warwick Publishing Inc., 1999.

Freeburg, Lloyd. *In the Bin*. Chicago: Triumph Books, 1998.

McDonnell, Chris (ed). *The Game I'll Never Forget*. Toronto: Firefly Books, 2002.

McFarlane, Brian. *Best of the Original Six*. Bolton, Ontario: Fenn Publishing Company Ltd., 2004.

Information was also used from the following print, broadcast and Internet media outlets:

Associated Press, *Bergen County Record*, *Boston Globe*, *Calgary Herald*, Canadian Press, canuckscentral.com, *CBC News: Disclosure*, *Chicago Daily Herald*, *Chicago Tribune*, davethehammerschultz.com, *Detroit Free Press*, *Detroit News*, *Edmonton Journal*, *Financial Post*, hockeydb. com, *Hockey Digest*, hockeydraftcentral.com, hockeyfights.com, legendsofhockey.blogspot.com, legendsofhockey.net, *La Presse*, *Los Angeles Times*, *Minneapolis Star Tribune*, *Montréal Gazette*, *National Post*, *New York Times*, nhl.com, nhlpa.com, *Ottawa Citizen*, *Prince George Citizen*, *Saskatoon Star Phoenix*, sportsnet.ca, tiedomi.com, *Toronto Star*, *Toronto Sun*, tsn.ca, *Vancouver Province*, *Vancouver Sun*, *Victoria Times Colonist*, *Washington Post*, *Windsor Star*, *Winnipeg Sun*.

Arpon Basu

Since he was eight years old, Arpon had been telling people he would one day make the National Hockey League. Any chance of that happening as a player, however, came to a crashing halt when, at age 15, Basu realized to his horror that he was completely devoid of any talent for the game. But he didn't give up, earning a graduate journalism degree from Concordia University and jumping straight to a sports writing job with the Canadian Press. The first time he walked into the Montréal Canadiens dressing room as a giddy cub reporter, Basu nearly fell over himself as it dawned on him that, despite his ineptitude on the ice, he had in fact been telling the truth as a dreamy-eyed eight-year-old. Arpon has also authored *Hockey's Hottest Players: The On- & Off-Ice Stories of the Superstars* for OverTime Books.